ANWAR SADAT

ANWAR SADAT

Patricia Aufderheide

CHELSEA HOUSE PUBLISHERS
NEW YORK
PHILADELPHIA

SENIOR EDITOR: William P. Hansen
ASSOCIATE EDITORS: John Haney
Richard Mandell
Marian W. Taylor
EDITORIAL COORDINATOR: Karyn Gullen Browne
EDITORIAL STAFF: Jennifer Caldwell
Juliette Dickstein
Perry Scott King
Tracy Tullis
ART DIRECTOR: Susan Lusk
LAYOUT: Irene Friedman
ART ASSISTANTS: Ghila Krajzman
Carol McDougall
Tenaz Mehta
COVER DESIGN: Jim Harter
PICTURE RESEARCH: Juliette Dickstein
Maureen Zent

3 5 7 9 8 6 4 2

Library of Congress Cataloging in Publication Data

Aufderheide, Patricia
Anwar Sadat.

(World leaders past & present)
Bibliography: p.
Includes index.
1. Sadat, Anwar, 1918–1981—Juvenile literature.
2. Egypt—Presidents—Biography.   I. Title.   II. Series.
DT107.828.S23A84   1985   962′.054′0924   [B]   85-3798
ISBN 0-87754-560-X
     0-7910-0600-X (pbk.)

Contents

John Adams
John Quincy Adams
Konrad Adenauer
Alexander the Great
Salvador Allende
Marc Antony
Corazon Aquino
Yasir Arafat
King Arthur
Hafez al-Assad
Kemal Atatürk
Attila
Clement Attlee
Augustus Caesar
Menachem Begin
David Ben-Gurion
Otto von Bismarck
Léon Blum
Simon Bolívar
Cesare Borgia
Willy Brandt
Leonid Brezhnev
Julius Caesar
John Calvin
Jimmy Carter
Fidel Castro
Catherine the Great
Charlemagne
Chiang Kai-Shek
Winston Churchill
Georges Clemenceau
Cleopatra
Constantine the Great
Hernán Cortés
Oliver Cromwell
Georges-Jacques
   Danton
Jefferson Davis
Moshe Dayan
Charles de Gaulle
Eamon De Valera
Eugene Debs
Deng Xiaoping
Benjamin Disraeli
Alexander Dubček
François & Jean-Claude
   Duvalier
Dwight Eisenhower
Eleanor of Aquitaine
Elizabeth I
Faisal
Ferdinand & Isabella
Francisco Franco
Benjamin Franklin

Frederick the Great
Indira Gandhi
Mohandas Gandhi
Giuseppe Garibaldi
Amin & Bashir Gemayel
Genghis Khan
William Gladstone
Mikhail Gorbachev
Ulysses S. Grant
Ernesto "Che" Guevara
Tenzin Gyatso
Alexander Hamilton
Dag Hammarskjöld
Henry VIII
Henry of Navarre
Paul von Hindenburg
Hirohito
Adolf Hitler
Ho Chi Minh
King Hussein
Ivan the Terrible
Andrew Jackson
James I
Wojciech Jaruzelski
Thomas Jefferson
Joan of Arc
Pope John XXIII
Pope John Paul II
Lyndon Johnson
Benito Juárez
John Kennedy
Robert Kennedy
Jomo Kenyatta
Ayatollah Khomeini
Nikita Khrushchev
Kim Il Sung
Martin Luther King, Jr.
Henry Kissinger
Kublai Khan
Lafayette
Robert E. Lee
Vladimir Lenin
Abraham Lincoln
David Lloyd George
Louis XIV
Martin Luther
Judas Maccabeus
James Madison
Nelson & Winnie
   Mandela
Mao Zedong
Ferdinand Marcos
George Marshall

Mary, Queen of Scots
Tomáš Masaryk
Golda Meir
Klemens von Metternich
James Monroe
Hosni Mubarak
Robert Mugabe
Benito Mussolini
Napoléon Bonaparte
Gamal Abdel Nasser
Jawaharlal Nehru
Nero
Nicholas II
Richard Nixon
Kwame Nkrumah
Daniel Ortega
Mohammed Reza Pahlavi
Thomas Paine
Charles Stewart
   Parnell
Pericles
Juan Perón
Peter the Great
Pol Pot
Muammar el-Qaddafi
Ronald Reagan
Cardinal Richelieu
Maximilien Robespierre
Eleanor Roosevelt
Franklin Roosevelt
Theodore Roosevelt
Anwar Sadat
Haile Selassie
Prince Sihanouk
Jan Smuts
Joseph Stalin
Sukarno
Sun Yat-sen
Tamerlane
Mother Teresa
Margaret Thatcher
Josip Broz Tito
Toussaint L'Ouverture
Leon Trotsky
Pierre Trudeau
Harry Truman
Queen Victoria
Lech Walesa
George Washington
Chaim Weizmann
Woodrow Wilson
Xerxes
Emiliano Zapata
Zhou Enlai

CHELSEA HOUSE PUBLISHERS

ON LEADERSHIP

Arthur M. Schlesinger, jr.

LEADERSHIP, it may be said, is really what makes the world go round. Love no doubt smooths the passage; but love is a private transaction between consenting adults. Leadership is a public transaction with history. The idea of leadership affirms the capacity of individuals to move, inspire and mobilize masses of people so that they act together in pursuit of an end. Sometimes leadership serves good purposes, sometimes bad; but whether the end is benign or evil, great leaders are those men and women who leave their personal stamp on history.

Now, the very concept of leadership implies the proposition that individuals can make a difference. This proposition has never been universally accepted. From classical times to the present day, eminent thinkers have regarded individuals as no more than the agents and pawns of larger forces, whether the gods and goddesses of the ancient world or, in the modern era, race, class, nation, the dialectic, the will of the people, the spirit of the times, history itself. Against such forces, the individual dwindles into insignificance.

So contends the thesis of historical determinism. Tolstoy's great novel *War and Peace* offers a famous statement of the case. Why, Tolstoy asked, did millions of men in the Napoleonic wars, denying their human feelings and their common sense, move back and forth across Europe slaughtering their fellows? "The war," Tolstoy answered, "was bound to happen simply because it was bound to happen." All prior history predetermined it. As for leaders, they, Tolstoy said, "are but the labels that serve to give a name to an end and, like labels, they have the least possible connection with the event." The greater the leader, "the more conspicuous the inevitability and the predestination of every act he commits." The leader, said Tolstoy, is "the slave of history."

Determinism takes many forms. Marxism is the determinism of class, Nazism the determinism of race. But the idea of men and women as the slaves of history runs athwart the deepest human instincts. Rigid determinism abolishes the idea of human freedom—the assumption of free choice that underlies every move we make, every word we speak, every thought we think. It abolishes the idea of human responsibility, since it is manifestly unfair to reward or punish people for actions that are by definition beyond their control. No one can live consistently by any deterministic creed. The Marxist states prove this themselves by their extreme susceptibility to the cult of leadership.

More than that, history refutes the idea that individuals make no difference. In December 1931 a British politician crossing Park Avenue in New York City between 76th and 77th Streets around ten-thirty at night looked in the wrong direction and was knocked down by an automobile—a moment, he later recalled, of a man aghast, a world aglare: "I do not understand why I was not broken like an eggshell or squashed like a gooseberry." Fourteen months later an American politician, sitting in an open car in Miami, Florida, was fired on by an assassin; the man beside him was hit. Those who believe that individuals make no difference to history might well ponder whether the next two decades would have been the same had Mario Contasini's car killed Winston Churchill in 1931 and Giuseppe Zangara's bullet killed Franklin Roosevelt in 1933. Suppose, in addition, that Adolf Hitler had been killed in the street fighting during the Munich *Putsch* of 1923 and that Lenin had died of typhus during the First World War. What would the 20th century be like now?

For better or for worse, individuals do make a difference. "The notion that a people can run itself and its affairs anonymously," wrote the philosopher William James, "is now well known to be the silliest of absurdities. Mankind does nothing save through initiatives on the part of inventors, great or small, and imitation by the rest of us—these are the sole factors in human progress. Individuals of genius show the way, and set the patterns, which common people then adopt and follow."

Leadership, James suggests, means leadership in thought as well as in action. In the long run, leaders in thought may well make the greater difference to the world. But, as Woodrow Wilson once said, "Those only are leaders of men, in the general eye, who lead in action. . . . It is at their hands that new thought gets its translation into the crude language of deeds." Leaders in thought often invent in solitude and obscurity, leaving to later generations the tasks of imitation. Leaders in action—the leaders portrayed in this series—have to be effective in their own time.

And they cannot be effective by themselves. They must act in response to the rhythms of their age. Their genius must be adapted, in a phrase of William James's, "to the receptivities of the moment." Leaders are useless without followers. "There goes the mob," said the French politician hearing a clamor in the streets. "I am their leader. I must follow them." Great leaders turn the inchoate emotions of the mob to purposes of their own. They seize on the opportunities of their time, the hopes, fears, frustrations, crises, potentialities.

They succeed when events have prepared the way for them, when the community is waiting to be aroused, when they can provide the clarifying and organizing ideas. Leadership ignites the circuit between the individual and the mass and thereby alters history.

It may alter history for better or for worse. Leaders have been responsible for the most extravagant follies and most monstrous crimes that have beset suffering humanity. They have also been vital in such gains as humanity has made in individual freedom, religious and racial tolerance, social justice and respect for human rights.

There is no sure way to tell in advance who is going to lead for good and who for evil. But a glance at the gallery of men and women in *World Leaders—Past and Present* suggests some useful tests.

One test is this: do leaders lead by force or by persuasion? By command or by consent? Through most of history leadership was exercised by the divine right of authority. The duty of followers was to defer and to obey. "Theirs not to reason why,/ Theirs but to do and die." On occasion, as with the so-called "enlightened despots" of the 18th century in Europe, absolutist leadership was animated by humane purposes. More often, absolutism nourished the passion for domination, land, gold and conquest and resulted in tyranny.

The great revolution of modern times has been the revolution of equality. The idea that all people should be equal in their legal condition has undermined the old structures of authority, hierarchy and deference. The revolution of equality has had two contrary effects on the nature of leadership. For equality, as Alexis de Tocqueville pointed out in his great study *Democracy in America*, might mean equality in servitude as well as equality in freedom.

"I know of only two methods of establishing equality in the political world," Tocqueville wrote. "Rights must be given to every citizen, or none at all to anyone . . . save one, who is the master of all." There was no middle ground "between the sovereignty of all and the absolute power of one man." In his astonishing prediction of 20th-century totalitarian dictatorship, Tocqueville explained how the revolution of equality could lead to the "*Führerprinzip*" and more terrible absolutism than the world had ever known.

But when rights are given to every citizen and the sovereignty of all is established, the problem of leadership takes a new form, becomes more exacting than ever before. It is easy to issue commands and enforce them by the rope and the stake, the concentration camp and the *gulag.* It is much harder to use argument and achievement to overcome opposition and win consent. The Founding Fathers of the United States understood the difficulty. They believed that history had given them the opportunity to decide, as

Alexander Hamilton wrote in the first Federalist Paper, whether men are indeed capable of basing government on "reflection and choice, or whether they are forever destined to depend . . . on accident and force."

Government by reflection and choice called for a new style of leadership and a new quality of followership. It required leaders to be responsive to popular concerns, and it required followers to be active and informed participants in the process. Democracy does not eliminate emotion from politics; sometimes it fosters demagoguery; but it is confident that, as the greatest of democratic leaders put it, you cannot fool all of the people all of the time. It measures leadership by results and retires those who overreach or falter or fail.

It is true that in the long run despots are measured by results too. But they can postpone the day of judgment, sometimes indefinitely, and in the meantime they can do infinite harm. It is also true that democracy is no guarantee of virtue and intelligence in government, for the voice of the people is not necessarily the voice of God. But democracy, by assuring the rights of opposition, offers built-in resistance to the evils inherent in absolutism. As the theologian Reinhold Niebuhr summed it up, "Man's capacity for justice makes democracy possible, but man's inclination to injustice makes democracy necessary."

A second test for leadership is the end for which power is sought. When leaders have as their goal the supremacy of a master race or the promotion of totalitarian revolution or the acquisition and exploitation of colonies or the protection of greed and privilege or the preservation of personal power, it is likely that their leadership will do little to advance the cause of humanity. When their goal is the abolition of slavery, the liberation of women, the enlargement of opportunity for the poor and powerless, the extension of equal rights to racial minorities, the defense of the freedoms of expression and opposition, it is likely that their leadership will increase the sum of human liberty and welfare.

Leaders have done great harm to the world. They have also conferred great benefits. You will find both sorts in this series. Even "good" leaders must be regarded with a certain wariness. Leaders are not demigods; they put on their trousers one leg after another just like ordinary mortals. No leader is infallible, and every leader needs to be reminded of this at regular intervals. Irreverence irritates leaders but is their salvation. Unquestioning submission corrupts leaders and demeans followers. Making a cult of a leader is always a mistake. Fortunately hero worship generates its own antidote. "Every hero," said Emerson, "becomes a bore at last."

The signal benefit the great leaders confer is to embolden the rest of us to live according to our own best selves, to be active, insistent, and resolute in affirming our own sense of things. For great leaders attest to the reality of human freedom against the supposed inevitabilities of history. And they attest to the wisdom and power that may lie within the most unlikely of us, which is why Abraham Lincoln remains the supreme example of great leadership. A great leader, said Emerson, exhibits new possibilities to all humanity. "We feed on genius. . . . Great men exist that there may be greater men."

Great leaders, in short, justify themselves by emancipating and empowering their followers. So humanity struggles to master its destiny, remembering with Alexis de Tocqueville: "It is true that around every man a fatal circle is traced beyond which he cannot pass; but within the wide verge of that circle he is powerful and free; as it is with man, so with communities."

—*New York*

1

Ancient Land, Modern Problems

It was October 6, 1981. Everyone in Egypt knew it was a special day—the repairman's little boy running down the alleys of a Cairo slum, clutching a penny for the morning bread; the woman architect choosing her outfit from a set of expensive suits in an eighth-floor apartment; the old woman stirring beans in a blackened pot in her village. They were all ready for a holiday.

Many people could remember the events of the same calendar day eight years earlier. On October 6, 1973, Egyptian forces had launched a surprise attack and crossed the Suez Canal to recapture land lost to Israel in the Six-Day War of June 1967. Everyone had said it could not be done.

So when President Anwar Sadat, the man who had planned "the Crossing," staged a gigantic military parade every year on that day, a large portion of the population of Cairo attended. In fact, no one had a better time at great occasions like this than Sadat himself. Early in the morning he began to prepare for this dramatic media event. He had probably eaten his usual light breakfast of papaya and honey, since he worried a lot about his diet and had a delicate stomach. Then he carefully inspected his elaborate uniform. He was a stylish

Anwar Sadat (1918–1981) became president of Egypt on the death of the nation's second president, Gamal Abdel Nasser (1918–1970).

Queen Cleopatra of Egypt (69 B.C.–30 B.C.) receives Mark Antony (83 B.C.–30 B.C.), commander of the eastern half of the Roman Empire. The story of their relationship as lovers and military allies, later inspired numerous works of literature, including Shakespeare's tragedy, *Antony and Cleopatra*.

A Cairo resident comforts her mourning friend during the funeral of Anwar Sadat. The assassination grieved many Americans, Israelis, and Europeans.

dresser and had an elegant bearing. In fact, he was once chosen by the Italian fashion industry as one of the ten best-dressed men in the world.

Upon his arrival at the parade ground, bodyguards clustered around the reviewing stand and made sure that his wife, Jihan, a half-English and very sophisticated lady, was safely enclosed in the glassed-in box behind him. The tanks, jeeps, and troops passed before him in perfect order. Suddenly things went terribly wrong. One of the jeeps screeched to a halt directly in front of Sadat. Soldiers jumped out, pointed their guns at him, and opened up with bursts of automatic fire. As Vice-President Hosni Mubarak looked on, stunned, Sadat crumpled. The assassins leaped back into their jeep and sped away from the bloody scene.

A nation's leader was dead, slain by Muslim fundamentalists who were members of an opposition faction within his own army. They thought he had betrayed them. It was a brutal and shocking act, but even harder to understand was the reaction at home and abroad. In the United States and Western Europe there was sadness and consternation. In most Arab countries, however, the media carried the news with joy, and there were even some public celebrations. In Egypt there was silence. It was as if the whole nation had shrugged its shoulders in complete indifference.

Many Western leaders attended the funeral. Three former presidents of the United States—Jimmy Carter, Gerald Ford, and Richard Nixon—as well as diplomat Henry Kissinger, were present for the brief ceremony. A mere handful of Arab leaders came; only Somalia, the Sudan, and Oman sent representatives. Ironically, Prime Minister Begin of Israel was there. Few Egyptians were watching; the streets were deserted as the funeral procession passed through Cairo on its way to a small cemetery on the outskirts of the capital.

Egyptian soldiers look on in stunned silence as Sadat's limousine, carrying their dying leader, his wounded secretary, and his bodyguards, speeds from the scene of the shooting.

The U.S. delegation to Sadat's funeral arrives in Cairo on October 9, 1981. Counterclockwise from top center are: former secretary of state Henry Kissinger (b. 1923); former president Gerald Ford (b. 1913); a security officer; former president Jimmy Carter (b. 1924) and his wife Rosalyn; and former president Richard Nixon (b. 1913).

Sadat was the leader of a nation of which Americans are largely ignorant. Most of us have a vague set of associations: the Pyramids, Cleopatra, mummies, the Nile. In fact, these associations, romantic images of Egypt's ancient past, remind us just how little we know of its history and present times.

Egypt sits on the far northeastern tip of Africa, where that continent meets southwest Asia. It is a hub of international activity. Running through the center of the country is the huge Nile River.

The valley and delta of the Nile are the most

fertile areas of Egypt. The rest of the country is mostly desert. As the river meanders north from the Sudan into the Mediterranean Sea, it brings life and work. Wherever the Nile flows, people are able to grow crops—traditionally cotton and wheat, as well as clover, vegetables, and fruits such as oranges and melons. Away from the Nile, the country is sparsely populated, inhabited mainly by nomads. Egypt, with its 363,000 square miles, is almost the size of France and Spain combined. Yet only the 4% of the land irrigated by the Nile can be farmed, and 98% of the population lives in that small area. In other words, almost all of Egypt's 43 million people inhabit an area smaller than the country of Denmark.

The Nile's rhythms and routes have set the terms of daily life in Egypt for thousands of years. Each year the peasant farmers known as *fellahin*

A Nile River boat, propelled by sail and oars, prepares to depart for a European-led expedition in the 1880s. The remains of Egypt's ancient civilization have long been a magnet for Western explorers and archaeologists.

planted crops to be harvested before September, when the Nile flooded. Each year the floods receded, leaving a layer of silt containing rich minerals for a new crop.

Much of this routine has changed now, for social and technical reasons. One of the main technical reasons was the building of the Aswan High Dam between 1956 and 1968. This huge structure dams up the Nile near Egypt's southern border, creating a vast reservoir called Lake Nasser. The dam controls the river's flow and eliminates floods. Agriculture has been modernized as a result; farmers now grow a greater variety of crops and use crop rotation to increase output. But the dam also has drawbacks. It has made it necessary for farmers to use expensive commercial fertilizers, it has increased the amount of salt in the soil, and it has contributed to the spread of a water-carried disease called schistosomiasis.

Construction of the Aswan High Dam was at midpoint in 1964. To provide irrigation for the more than 1 million acres of farmland, the Nile River was diverted into a new channel that had been carved into a bed of solid granite.

Many of the recent social changes in Egypt can be credited to the man for whom the dam's lake was named, Gamal Abdel Nasser. President of Egypt from 1956 to 1970, he came to power when 2% of the population owned at least half the land. Most people lived in the countryside, in villages of 20,000 to 30,000 inhabitants. Most were peasants, who worked the fields under the watchful eye of foremen carrying umbrellas or parasols to ward off the relentless sun. The peasants paid heavy taxes to both landlords and government officials.

When Nasser took office, he made it illegal to hold large tracts of land and made it easy for peasants to own small parcels of land. For the first time in thousands of years, Egyptian *fellahin* became landowners. It is no wonder that Nasser's picture can still be found in many Egyptian homes.

The Nile divides Egypt as much as it unites it. South of the city of Cairo, people have always

Egypt is perhaps best symbolized to Western nations by the great pyramids of Giza. Built in the desert almost 3,000 years before the birth of Christ, these enormous stone structures enclose the tombs of early Egyptian kings.

Travelers cross Egypt's vast, sandy wastes by camel. Sometimes called "ships of the desert," camels have been used for transportation and farm work for centuries.

lived and worked in a strip of land between 5 and 20 miles wide, and, when they died, have been buried in the desert just beyond. The dry climate has preserved their remains so well that historians and archaeologists know much more about their death rituals than their lives. (For a long time, many people thought the Egyptians were especially obsessed with death because of this accident of research.) North of Cairo the Nile spreads out into a delta, where people have vigorously traded in Mediterranean commerce for thousands of years; beneath its muddy soil lies hidden much of the remains of their history.

This delta area fostered one of mankind's earliest civilizations. For 3,000 years Egypt was ruled by great dynasties of pharaohs, or kings. In the 6th century B.C., invading Persians conquered the entire area. Persian rule in Egypt came to an end in 332 B.C., following the defeat of the Persians by Alexander the Great. For the next three hundred years Egypt was ruled by the successors to Ptolemy, the Greek general to whom Alexander had granted authority over Egypt upon his death. When

Queen Cleopatra of Egypt, the last of the Ptolemies, died in the 1st century B.C., Egypt became a Roman province, and was governed from Rome until the division of the Roman Empire in A.D. 395. After that Egypt was governed from Constantinople (modern-day Istanbul) as a province of the Roman Empire in the East (also known as the Byzantine Empire). Roman rule in Egypt came to an end in A.D. 642, when Patriarch Gregory, the governor of Alexandria, the last city in Egypt to have held out against invading Muslim Arabs, finally decided to surrender the whole country to the invaders.

Egypt then took on a new role as a center and leader of the Arab world. Arabs are people who have in common the Arabic language originally spread by the desert people of the Arabian peninsula. It was the language of the prophet Muhammad, who founded the Islamic religion in the 7th

An Egyptian woman dances during celebrations marking the birthday of Muhammad (570–632), the Arab prophet who established the Islamic, or Muslim, religion. The majority of modern Egyptians profess the Islamic faith.

General Mikhail Skobelev (1843–1882) accepts the surrender of General Osman Pasha (1832–1900) in Constantinople (modern Istanbul) at the conclusion of the last Russo-Turkish War (1877–1878). Despite this defeat, the Turkish Ottoman Empire continued to control Egypt until 1914, when it officially became a British protectorate.

century. Islam teaches that there is only one God, Allah, whom everyone should worship in simple daily rites. Muslims believe that Moses and Jesus were great prophets; but they do not believe that Jesus was the son of God, any more than Muhammad himself was.

After the death of Muhammad, in A.D. 632, Islam spread throughout Asia and Africa. One of the first areas where it was adopted wholeheartedly was Egypt. Previously, most Egyptians had practiced a version of Christianity called Coptic. (Even today, around 10% of Egyptians are Coptic Christians.) Possibly because they found their Christian rulers too harsh and the taxes imposed on them too high, many Egyptians enthusiastically adopted Islam, a religion that stresses equality.

Between 642 and 1517, Egypt was ruled by a succession of Arab dynasties. In 1517 the country was overrun by the Ottoman Turks, who had become the dominant power in the Middle East after conquering Constantinople in 1453. Egypt remained part of the Ottoman Empire for four centuries until the outbreak of World War I.

To the many peoples converted to Islam, Egypt brought a huge settled population and the sophistication of an ancient culture. It soon became a major center of learning. Cairo's university, al-Azhar, which functions to this day, was founded in the 10th century. Today a third of all Arabs live in Egypt, which for many years was the center of the organization representing all the Arab countries, the Arab League.

Born in a country which had long held a leading position in the Arab world, at a time when Ottoman influence was on the verge of extinction and the European presence in the Middle East was beginning to be resented by the Arab peoples, Anwar Sadat grew to manhood during a period when the seeds of a new Arab awareness were being sown. The Arab world was about to make its mark on the 20th century.

Founded in 969, al-Azhar, the Muslim university in Cairo, is the world's oldest institution of higher education. Specializing in Islamic studies, it contains an Arabic library unsurpassed anywhere.

2

A Log Cabin in Egypt

Anwar Sadat was proud of having been born and raised in a Nile delta village. He felt that his humble origins qualified him to speak for the great majority of Egyptians. In fact, he came to feel that his own life story and that of Egypt was "one and the same thing," as he put it in his autobiography, *In Search of Identity.* When *Time* magazine chose him as Man of the Year in 1978, he compared himself to Abraham Lincoln. "Lincoln was a villager too," he said, "and he moved alone."

Sadat was born in 1918 in Mit Abul Kom, a village about 40 miles north of Cairo. The village was in an area of rich farmland, and his family was well respected, partly because his father, a clerk in a military hospital, had completed grade school.

Still, the respect of fellow villagers—who honored Sadat's father with the title *effendi* (much like saying "professor" or "your honor")—did not supply the family with money. There were 13 children in the family, and a civil servant was not paid much. Young Anwar lived much like other children in the village, helping with the farm work and household chores. At the local school, he was not a particularly good student and often could not keep his mind on his work. He was a daydreamer. And

Cairo, Egypt's capital, abounds with mosques, which are Muslim places of worship. An essential part of any mosque is its minaret, a tall, slender tower from which the faithful are called to prayer every day.

Anwar Sadat was named Man of the Year by *Time* magazine in 1978; in the same year, he shared the Nobel Peace Prize with Israeli premier Menachem Begin (b. 1913).

Muhammad Ali (1769– 1849) ruled Egypt for 43 years, beginning in 1805. Although he taxed the impoverished Egyptian people unmercifully and was often cruel, he also supported education, the expansion of scientific learning, and trade.

one thing he dreamed about was playing a heroic part in a revolution to free Egypt.

When Sadat was a boy, Egypt was under the sway of British colonialism. This situation had evolved gradually. At the beginning of the 19th century, Egypt had been part of the Ottoman Empire. In 1805 a Turkish army officer, Muhammad Ali, seized power from the Ottoman governor in Egypt. In 1841 he was declared the hereditary ruler of Egypt, and only nominally subject to Ottoman authority.

Ali was eager to turn Egypt into a modern state. One of his plans was to build a canal linking the Mediterranean Sea to the Red Sea at the Gulf of Suez. The Ottoman Empire was too weak to stop him, and both the British and French governments took an interest in the project. The French eventually helped build the canal, which was opened in 1869. They also won a 99-year concession to run it. But the British, who saw Egypt as the front door to India, their most important colony, did not want to leave their French rivals in control of such an important commercial and strategic asset as the canal.

By 1875 the British had persuaded Egypt's ruler, Ismail (Muhammad Ali's grandson), to sell them his 44% share in the canal; he had readily agreed because Egypt's treasury was empty at the time. Following this deal, France and England divided control of the country between them, with-

A crowd assembles to watch the first passage of merchant vessels through the new Suez Canal. The great artificial waterway between the Mediterranean and the Red Sea opened in 1869.

out formally declaring it a colony. Finally, when it seemed that a military revolt against Ismail's successor might give Egypt full political independence from Ottoman authority, British troops landed in Egypt in 1882 and defeated the rebels. This was the beginning of the British occupation of Egypt, which continued until the final withdrawal of British troops in 1954. During this time Egypt was called "The Veiled Protectorate" because the British exercised full control while pretending only to offer advice and aid.

When Sadat was still a toddler carrying jars of molasses for his grandmother, other Egyptians were rocking the country with acts of rebellion. In 1920, a year after a nationalist political party called *Wafd* was formed, there was a nationwide uprising against the British. It failed but the independence movement grew. Clashes between the British and the Egyptians continued, and one of them created

> *When he was still in grade school Anwar began dressing up in a white sheet like Gandhi, and he would walk through the village leading a goat on a string. Then he would go and sit under a tree, pretending he did not want to eat.*
>
> —SEKINA SADAT
> Anwar Sadat's sister

Mohandas K. Gandhi (1869–1948), the leading Indian nationalist who guided his country to independence from the British in 1947, had a strong influence on the young Sadat.

a martyr whom Sadat, as a boy and a man, greatly revered.

His name was Zahran. Like Sadat, he had been born and raised in a delta village on the Nile. And like many other Egyptians, he hated the sight of British troops. One day British soldiers were amusing themselves by shooting pigeons near Zahran's village, and they accidentally set a wheat silo on fire. The incident sparked a riot in which a British captain was killed. Through an Egyptian court, the British sentenced four Egyptians to death. Zahran, the first to be hanged, became a national hero. In later years, when he himself feared for his life, Sadat cherished the memory of Zahran walking nobly to the scaffold.

Another hero of Sadat's youth was Kemal Atatürk, the brilliant Turkish military and political leader who had engineered the downfall of the Ottomans. With Atatürk in charge, Turkey had been declared a republic in 1923, and the last Ottoman caliph was sent into exile in the following year, thus ending centuries of religious and dynastic rule.

Young Sadat also revered the Indian independence leader Mohandas Gandhi (known as the Mahatma, or Great Soul). In 1932, when Sadat was 14, Gandhi toured Egypt, talking about nonviolence as a way to combat injustice. Sadat was impressed and quickly tried to imitate him. He climbed to the roof of his parents' house, took off his clothes, and put on an apron in an attempt to look more like Gandhi, who wore a simple white robe. When his father warned him that he might catch pneumonia, he came down from the roof. But he had already demonstrated his ability to appreciate the dramatic power of an image. Apparently he found Gandhi's image more important than his doctrines, because Sadat soon became involved in protest that was anything but nonviolent.

There was yet another hero for young Sadat: Adolf Hitler, the new leader of Nazi Germany. Sadat knew little of Germany but, like many young Egyptians, was impressed by Hitler because he saw in him a potential challenge to Britain.

Kemal Atatürk (1881–1938) was the first president of the Republic of Turkey, the secular state that he helped to establish in 1923 following the overthrow of Ottoman rule. Atatürk, whose memory Sadat greatly revered, introduced many reforms, including the outlawing of polygamy and the creation of modern civil and criminal legal codes.

Eventually, the Sadat family moved to Cairo, where Anwar went to high school. Though not a particularly good student, he finally got his diploma at the age of 18. Along with other students, he joined in anti-British demonstrations, burning train cars and chanting slogans for the restoration of independence. At this stage in Egyptian history, the main issue underlying the general debate about independence was the country's constitution. As it stood in 1923 it granted, technically at least, a measure of independence.

The prospect of even partial independence, however, disappeared in 1924, when Sir Lee Stack, the British commander of the Egyptian army, was murdered by a fanatical member of the Wafd party. The British response was swift and stern. They again reserved to themselves high positions in the Egyptian administration, and continued to hold the authority which they had intended to grant to

German dictator Adolf Hitler (1889–1945) was an unlikely object of Sadat's tendency toward hero worship, but the idealistic young Egyptian, who knew little about the violent and bloody regime of the Nazi leader, admired Hitler for his defiance of the British.

Attendants at a Cairo mosque provide visiting British tourists with special overshoes during the 1920s, thus ensuring complete observance of the Muslim rules for correct deportment in a place of worship.

Egyptian officials under the terms of the 1923 constitution.

Although Sadat knew little of the details of this constitution, he committed himself whole-heartedly to the struggle for its restoration. Just as he had paid more attention to Gandhi's image than to his doctrines, Sadat, in this early period of his life, was more concerned with action than with details. In 1936, thanks in part to the British, Sadat got a lucky break—a chance to improve his education.

The Wafd party struck a deal with the British to modernize the Egyptian army and improve Egypt's defenses. A military academy was established, and Sadat was one of the many young men who flocked to it. There he studied Egyptian history in detail and learned to analyze battles, wars, and revolutions. He even studied the Battle of Gettysburg, the turning point of the American Civil War.

3

Husband, Soldier, Terrorist

*The dogmas of Islam must
be inculcated into all
branches of the army.*
—ANWAR SADAT
writing during the 1940s, when he was
a member of the Free Officers

Anwar Sadat was raised with one foot in ancient village traditions and the other in crisis-ridden modern times. He would later express his feelings in an almost poetical way when thinking of his peasant background. "I can never lose my way," he once said, "because I know I have living roots there, deep down in the soil."

He did indeed have living roots, in the form of a family he left behind as he moved ever further away from peasant life. At about the same time that he started his military training he married. His bride had been found for him by his parents, in accordance with the Egyptian tradition of arranged marriages. By the time he was 24 he had three daughters. He also had many doubts about the suitability, for a young officer in a modern army, of a wife whom he had married according to old customs. Sadat was beginning to realize that Egypt itself, and not just its army, would have to be modernized.

He had little time, however, to think about his marriage problems. Soon after graduating from the military academy, he was sent to a distant outpost, along with a group of other young officers. Among them was a young man named Gamal Abdel Nasser, who was the same age as Sadat and had a similar background. He too had taken part

Sadat had long dreamed of an Egypt independent from Britain. In later years, he was amused by the irony of his acceptance in the British-controlled military academy. "The British helped me to join," he noted, "when the reason I wanted to join...was to kick them out of Egypt."

The Nile delta forms a backdrop for this view of modern Cairo, much of which looks today as it did centuries ago. Sadat's family moved to the Egyptian capital when he was a teenager.

in demonstrations and, during his time in the military academy, had studied battles of independence. "We have said several times we are going to wake the nation from its sleep," he wrote to a friend at the age of 21, "but alas so far nothing has been carried out."

Sadat, Nasser, and other ambitious young officers would sit around fires late at night discussing future possibilities. Eventually, they formed a revolutionary group called the Free Officers Organization. It was in that lonely outpost that plans were made for an eventual takeover of Egypt in the name of its *fellahin*. The officers, who foresaw a modern, professional government for Egypt, run by people like themselves, were united by their hatred of the British, by their training, and by their sense of brotherhood with the other peoples of the Arab world.

Egypt was not the only Arab country that had fallen under the shadow of European power. In reaction to this situation, all over the Arab world, an "Arab Awakening"—a sense of common cause and identity—was growing. The roots of the continuing struggles for independence throughout the region lay in the collapse of the Ottoman Empire during World War I.

Two British actions at that time are remembered by Arabs to this day as betrayals. One was the Sykes-Picot Agreement. When war broke out in 1914 the British government had promised that if

British foreign secretary Arthur Balfour (second from left; 1848–1930) arrives in Washington, D.C., in 1917 to discuss Allied strategy. Balfour's decision in that same year to support Jewish aspirations for a homeland in Palestine disturbed many Arabs.

Arab soldiers fought on the side of the Allies, then Britain would help the Arab countries achieve independence following the war. Instead, in the 1916 Sykes-Picot Agreement, Britain, France, and Russia divided the entire region among themselves, establishing a number of "mandates," or colonies.

A year later, the British foreign secretary, Sir Arthur Balfour, after meeting with Jewish leaders, announced the Balfour Declaration, which pledged that Britain would work for "the establishment in Palestine of a national home for the Jewish people." In the opinion of many Arabs, this amounted to inviting new settlers to invade those very lands where they themselves were denied nationhood.

Palestine, however, had long been a land in dispute. The Hebrews had settled in the area 2,000 years before the birth of Jesus and had gained control of the region in the 12th century B.C. Their kingdom lasted (with interruptions) until the Romans invaded the area three generations before Christ. The Jews rebelled against the Romans on many occasions, and each time the Romans retaliated by expelling the troublemakers. They moved one whole group, for instance, to the Egyptian city of Alexandria. The Jews, some of whom had turned to trading, dispersed throughout the world in the

Jews gather at the sacred Wailing Wall in Jerusalem, the city in Palestine also considered holy by Muslims and Christians. After the 1917 Balfour Declaration, the arrival in Palestine of increasing numbers of Jewish immigrants triggered deep resentment among Arab nationalists.

U.S. president Franklin D. Roosevelt (1882–1945) meets in Cairo with Egypt's King Farouk I (1920–1965), in 1945. Roosevelt's attempt to maintain cordial relations with both Arabs and Jews failed when he announced his sympathy for the Zionist movement, thus alienating many Arabs.

migrations known as "The Diaspora," a Greek word which means "scattering."

In many countries, the Jews, who maintained their own identity, were blamed for political problems and suffered much persecution. During the 19th century a political movement blossomed among Jews, reflecting their wish to return to the ancient source of their culture in Palestine. It was this movement, known as Zionism, which the British had recognized in the Balfour Declaration. Numbers of Jews had begun returning to Palestine long before the Balfour Declaration; after it the number increased, although the British tried to limit immigration.

The British betrayal of Arab nationalism, combined with their halfhearted recognition of Jewish claims in Palestine, created a bond of solidarity among Arab freedom fighters. It also sowed the seeds of bloody turmoil in the Middle East later in the century.

As World War II raged, young Egyptian officers made plans to strike out at the British close to home. In the summer of 1942, forces under General Erwin Rommel, the German commander in North Africa, reached the Egyptian fort at Alamein, only 65 miles from Alexandria. Many Egyptians welcomed them. In the streets of Cairo, crowds gathered to demonstrate, shouting pro-Rommel slogans. Sadat and his friends tried to get word to Rommel that they were anxious to work with him.

But this was the beginning of a run of bad luck for Sadat. First, the message failed to arrive. Then, when Sadat attempted to deliver into German hands an Egyptian general who had been dismissed by the British, the car in which they were traveling broke down. The final blow came when he and his fellow conspirators conducted a highly incompetent spying mission, which not only failed to further Egypt's fortunes but got the participants arrested.

Sadat spent two years in jail. Although he had begun his sentence with images of the heroic peasant Zahran in his head, the boredom of imprisonment eventually set in. Fortunately, however, he was only under light detention and escaped during one of his outings. He spent the next few months working at odd jobs.

His time in prison had not dampened his enthusiastic commitment to the creation of an independent, modern Egypt. King Farouk, who then ruled Egypt with English support, inspired little loyalty among his subjects. After the war, Egyptians continued to suffer. Against a background of inflation, which the government could not control, unfair taxes were imposed, while prices rose twice as fast as wages.

It was a time when extreme actions seemed logical to many, and especially to young military men. One favored method was terrorism. Sadat suggested blowing up the British embassy, only to have Nasser promptly veto the idea. Nasser, however, did not stop Sadat from helping plan the killing of an Egyptian official named Amin Osman Pasha, a former minister of finance who worked closely with the British. As a result Sadat was again jailed for two years. This time he was confined in a cold, dank cell, where at first he was not even permitted to read. Once allowed books, he became a diligent student, learning among other things French and English. The long months of imprisonment, although unpleasant, gave Sadat a great opportunity to think about past mistakes and future plans. One of his first decisions was to divorce his wife.

With cultural roots that date back to the fifth millenium B.C. the Egyptian people never lose their sense of identity, however hard the circumstances may be.
—ANWAR SADAT

American Jews demonstrate their support for unlimited Jewish immigration into Palestine in New York City in 1945. Despairing of British cooperation, the Zionist movement made strenuous efforts to gain U.S. backing for the establishment of a Jewish state in Palestine.

4

A War and a Revolution

While in prison Sadat heard that war had broken out between Israel and its Arab neighbors on May 15, 1948. It had been expected for some time. Shortly after World War II the newly organized United Nations had studied the best way in which to accede to Arab wishes and also to honor the promises contained in the Balfour Declaration. It was finally proposed that Palestine be divided into two separate states, one for Arabs and one for Jews, with a small area in the southwest, known as the Gaza Strip, to be controlled by Egypt. Jerusalem was to be an international city.

The Jews of Palestine accepted this proposal but the Arab leaders hated the idea, and continued to hope that one of the European powers would step in and block the creation of a new Jewish state. Two days after Israel formally achieved status as a nation, Egypt, Iraq, Lebanon, Syria, and Transjordan attacked.

Hundreds of thousands of Palestinian Arabs, fearing for their safety and terrified by the fighting, became refugees. The fears of some Eygptian army officers that the Arabs were not sufficiently well organized to win were soon realized. In fact, Israel won territory which the United Nations had originally intended to be used for an Arab state in Palestine.

Hoping to reduce confrontation between Arabs and Jews in Jerusalem, departing British troops laid a thicket of coiled barbed wire in the international city's streets on May 13, 1948. Three days later, Arab forces attacked the State of Israel.

Sadat's military virtues, courage and coolness, loyalty and devotion, force of character and disinterestedness and finally his love of justice, destined him to play a leading role in the Egyptian revolution of July 23, 1952.
—GAMAL ABDEL NASSER

British soldiers man an antiaircraft gun near the Suez Canal. A 1936 treaty between Britain and Egypt permitted the British to maintain a 10,000-man defense force in Egypt.

One of the people wounded during this war was Gamal Abdel Nasser. It was then that he concluded that Egypt's fate was linked with that of other Arab countries. "Is it possible," he wrote, "for us to overlook the fact that around us lies an Arab circle, and that this circle is as much a part of us as we are a part of it, that our history has been merged with it and that its interests are linked with ours?"

This reality, of which Nasser became increasingly convinced, had been ignored for years by the majority of Egyptians, who felt that their culture was much older and richer than that of many other Arab states, especially those desert kingdoms where seminomadic peoples had dominated. Egypt, as the largest Arab country, was generally distrusted by the other Arab nations. Now, faced with what they saw as a Jewish invasion of a traditionally Arab area, and which, moreover, had occasioned the flight of some of the Arab residents of Palestine, the Arab nations united in their opposition to Israel.

When Anwar Sadat was finally freed from prison he did not—as did so many young men—rush off to enlist. Instead, he bought some fashionable clothes and went to a health spa. His pride

Surrounded by their meager possessions, Palestinian Arabs uprooted by the 1948 war await relocation to the Egyptian-controlled Gaza strip. Nearly one million Palestinian Arabs were driven from their homes during the war.

Prior to leaving Palestine in early 1948, British troops prepare to aid a Jewish settlement besieged by Arab guerrillas. Such harassment of Jewish communities turned into all-out war following the foundation of the State of Israel, when the regular forces of five Arab nations launched an attack on the Jewish homeland.

In an atmosphere of mounting tension over the promised evacuation of British troops, Egyptian militiawomen practice firing British-made Enfield rifles in 1951. The disagreement about which nation owned the Suez Canal led to armed conflict between Britain and Egypt in 1956.

in his appearance was to continue throughout his life, as was his concern with health.

Since he had no profession, he began to consider what he might do to make a living, finally deciding to seek employment as an actor. He took out an ad in a Cairo magazine, which read, "I am a dark youth, 1.69 meters tall, 31 years old. I go in for comic acting, and I am ready to play any role in the theater or cinema. Anwar Sadat." This led to a job on the Cairo stage, where he appeared in a comedy.

Prime Minister Gamal Abdel Nasser (1918–1970) waves to a cheering crowd from his office window in 1954, following the Egyptian government's announcement that it had secured guarantees of British military withdrawal from the Suez Canal Zone. Nasser was to prove both popular and efficient as his nation's leader.

It was in prison that beauty became my presiding ideal and my idealism a perpetual craving for beauty, inspired by paramount desire to save Egypt from her besetting troubles and to help her advance toward perfection and beauty.

—ANWAR SADAT

Sadat also began to put his personal life back in order, arranging for his divorce and seeking new ways to make money. He went into business with an old friend and made several profitable deals in the course of the partnership. It was also at this time that he was introduced to a cousin of his partner's—an attractive girl of 15 named Jihan, who was half-English. Since she was interested in politics, she naturally found Sadat's stories of rebellion and imprisonment enthralling. They quickly decided to get married but first had to overcome her parents' objections. Not only had Sadat been involved in dangerous politics, but he was also very dark-skinned. Many Egyptians share a common Arab prejudice concerning darker skin. Jihan, however, a strong-willed person, finally persuaded her father to consent to the marriage.

On contacting Nasser again, Sadat discovered that the Free Officers were planning to overthrow King Farouk. The organization had grown considerably since the time Sadat had first become involved with it. Secrecy was maintained very carefully, and Nasser, now the head of the organization, was keeping his plans to himself.

In January 1952 British troops attacked a rebellious Egyptian police garrison in the town of Ismailia, which led to a rash of rioting in Cairo. Mobs expressed their anger and frustration by attacking the symbols of luxury that typified King Farouk's corrupt regime, such as expensive hotels, clubs, and movie houses. The king was rapidly losing control of the situation, and Egypt was obviously on the brink of revolution.

The Free Officers decided that unless they acted immediately, they might never have such a favorable opportunity again. Their schedule was moved up, an event which caught Sadat unprepared. On July 22, arriving home from the movies, he found a message from Nasser directing him to join the officers at once. Overnight, troops massed throughout Cairo, while Sadat drove frantically from one checkpoint to another in an attempt to find his comrades. Finally he found someone who knew him.

Sadat discovered that he had made contact not a moment too soon. Nasser wanted him to make the radio announcement of the coup, which was eventually broadcast at 7 a.m. on July 23, 1952. This was the beginning of Sadat's career as Nasser's public relations minister. Following the announcement of the change of government, he went home to his wife, who was at first angry with him for having stayed out all night. "Listen to the radio!" he told her in explanation.

Sadat was then given the task of flying to Alexandria to supervise the abdication of King Farouk on July 26. Sadat would write later: "From the bridge of the destroyer, I watched Farouk pass into the twilight of history. The sailors round me were jubilant."

The easy part was now over. It is often harder to govern than to win a revolution, and the most immediate problem facing the new regime was what to do with the supporters of the old government. Most members of the previous administration were still alive, since the coup had been quite bloodless. Many officers in Nasser's inner circle, Sadat included, demanded a purge of the old regime, and wanted Nasser to assume the powers of a dictator. But this was not to be. Nasser fully supported the democratic ideal and successfully held out against the combined wishes of his fellow commanders. He hoped to secure for the people of Egypt peace and prosperity on a scale they had never known before. He firmly believed that this could be achieved by an honest, efficient, and democratic government.

I respected Anwar Sadat because he was so dedicated—this is the main thing that attracted me. He was not a rich man, he was not good looking, he was not from a very high family. It was his personality.
—JIHAN SADAT

Supported by tanks and artillery, Egyptian troops surround King Farouk's palace in Cairo in 1952 during the coup that overthrew the monarchy.

5

"Yes, Yes, My President"

Sadat's announcement ushered in great changes both inside and outside Egypt. The regime that came to power in 1952, and which lasted until Nasser's death in 1970, raised Egypt to the fore-front of nonaligned nations, those countries which did not position themselves in the immediate camp of the Soviet Union or the United States.

Nasser stood for independence, both from foreign control and from domination by the country's wealthy elite. By 1954 he had finally managed to secure the complete withdrawal of British troops from Egypt. He played off the superpowers against each other, accepting aid from communists and capitalists alike. (Egypt, because of its strategic location, continued to receive as much attention from the modern powers as it had from earlier empires.)

Nasser played this dangerous game well, occasionally at no small cost to himself. In 1956, for instance, several Western nations, in cooperation with a number of international banks and aid agencies, offered to help finance the massive Aswan High Dam project. Nasser accepted this economic aid gratefully. When a confrontation with Israeli forces in February 1956 went badly for Egypt, Nasser began to appreciate the extent of Egypt's need for additional military aid. But the United States, a

Gamal Nasser (at left), who became Egypt's president in 1956, was to serve in that capacity for 14 years. Here, in 1965, he is officially notified by Anwar Sadat (at right) of his nomination for a third term.

The Egyptian government's decision to nationalize the Suez Canal, a vital trade link between the Americas, Europe, and Asia, immediately brought it into confrontation with the British and French, who had controlled the waterway for almost a century.

45

major arms supplier, refused such aid without special agreements. Nasser, not wishing to compromise Egypt's independence, eagerly accepted a Soviet offer of military aid a short time later. Finally, when he also officially recognized China, another communist power, the United States, outraged, persuaded the Western nations to cancel their loans for the Aswan project. Deeply offended by the Western attempt to dictate his country's political alignment, Nasser nationalized the Suez Canal, removing it from British and French control. This deprived Britain and France of the revenues they had been collecting on the canal since the 19th century.

Nasser then ordered that profits from the canal be used to finance the construction at Aswan. In October 1956 the Israelis, aided by French and British forces, captured the Gaza Strip and all of the Sinai Peninsula. The French and British

A cheering crowd of Cairenes, many lofting banners inscribed in praise of their leader, celebrates Nasser's 1956 announcement that he had nationalized the Suez Canal.

Under construction seven years, by 1967 the Aswan High Dam was near completion. Nasser used revenues from the nationalized Suez Canal to finance the billion-dollar project.

withdrew after two months, under heavy pressure from the United States, whose president, Dwight Eisenhower, was becoming increasingly concerned over the possibility of a general war involving the Soviets. American pressure was maintained until the Israelis finally pulled back in March 1957, thus losing to diplomacy what they had managed to win in war.

This conflict made Nasser a hero in the eyes of the nonaligned world. Egypt had emerged victorious on the diplomatic front, retaining its hold on a former Anglo-French imperial asset with the indirect support of a superpower supposedly sympathetic toward the previous owners. Taking advantage of his popularity, he turned his talk of Arab unity into fact, forming an alliance with Syria, following which the two countries became known as the United Arab Republic.

Soviet premier Nikita Khrushchev (1894–1971) joins Egyptian president Gamal Abdel Nasser in a symbolic handshake in New York City in 1960. Eager to increase its influence in the strategically important Mideast, the Soviet Union was happy to provide Egypt with economic and military aid.

Independence under Nasser also changed the situation inside Egypt. The government began taking measures intended directly to benefit the great majority of people, instituting health plans, for instance, and establishing many government-owned industries through which Egypt's economy was to be expanded and the resulting profits returned to the people. The prices of basic foods were kept low. The most dramatic departure from tradition came when Nasser forced landowners to break up their huge holdings. He limited ownership to 200 acres and made it easy for small farmers to acquire their own plots. Egypt, it seemed, was fast ceasing to be a culture that had more in common with the Middle Ages than the 20th century.

The skyline of Cairo was also changing rapidly as high-rise buildings soared above the ancient mosques. One of these imposing edifices was the 28-story building that housed the Ministry of Information, headquarters of the government-censored national radio and press. Although Nasser's regime ran the country in the name of the Egyptian people, there was little evidence of government by the people, despite the existence of parliamentary trappings and Nasser's initial enthusiasm for democratic principles. Government by dictatorship had emerged in Egypt. Nasser, backed by the military officers who formed the core of the Arab Socialist Union party, was becoming increasingly distrustful of people with ideas opposed to his own.

Anwar Sadat was one of the few people who remained unswervingly loyal to Nasser while he remained in power. It was reported by one journalist that Nasser gave Sadat the nickname of "Bikbashi Sah," or "Major Yes Yes." The same journalist also reported that Nasser once said, "If he would occasionally vary his way of expressing agreement, instead of forever saying 'Sah' (Yes, sir), that would be easier on my nerves." But Nasser was prepared to put up with this servility, since he had great respect for Sadat's ability to present any viewpoint with apparent conviction and conspicuous flair.

Sadat made two particularly important contributions to the Nasser regime: he gained public support for government policies, and he improved Nasser's image. Sadat, who had named his only son after his boss, wrote a children's book in which he spoke of Nasser not just in heroic terms, but in terms usually reserved for gods. "Gamal, O Lord," he wrote, "is your magnificent creation, your conquering genius, your true servant." He went on, "Gamal Abdel Nasser, whose name I gave you, my son, is my friend, my child, whom I have loved and respected since we were junior officers in 1938."

In this book, Sadat also noted clearly who his friends and enemies were, calling the Americans colonialists while praising the Soviet Union. He made comparisons between America and Israel, stating, "America's goal, like Zionism's, is world domination." Israel, he wrote, had taken power in a way that would "make humanity blush with shame." For Sadat, a hero-worshipper, Nasser was an ideal figure. In fact, Sadat's respect for the heroes of his youth stayed with him. As late as 1953, when he was already a member of the ruling Revolutionary Command Council, he wrote favorably of Adolf Hitler, whom he praised for challenging Britain and restoring national pride.

It is not nearly as difficult to explain his love for Nasser. In the years from 1956 to 1964 Egypt took giant strides forward. Average income increased and education improved. During the 1950s two new schools opened every three days. Egyptians were increasingly being trained as engineers, scientists, lawyers, doctors, and teachers. It seemed that both the dream of national progress and the vision of Arab unity might yet be realized under Nasser's steady rule.

Along with growth, however, some problems persisted and multiplied. Population growth increased; while cities swelled, farmland shrank. Land reform was only partially effective, with the presence of big landowners only being limited, rather than completely eliminated. In fact, by the end of Nasser's regime, fewer peasants owned land than at the beginning. Only the growth of poverty had been slowed. Whenever privately owned and govern-

Visiting New York City in 1960, Gamal Nasser greets Cuban head of state Fidel Castro (b. 1926). Cuba and Egypt were, at that time, among the most influential members of the group of nations that aligned themselves with neither the United States nor the Soviet Union.

ment-owned industries found themselves working side by side, corruption quickly characterized the relationship, as government officials had many opportunities to strike secret deals with private businesses. Problems also arose in the armed forces, as military leaders became less dedicated to their original ideals. As the economy grew stagnant, the government was forced to expand its own bureaucracy to provide employment for the increasing numbers of educated Egyptians for whom there were no jobs.

The situation in the Arab world became even more confused when Britain gave its backing to King Hussein of Jordan, and the United States sent marines to support Christian fighters in Lebanon in 1958. Arab unity also began to crumble. After an internal coup Syria seceded from the United Arab Republic in 1962.

To bolster his position as an Arab leader and to encourage populist rather than conservative leadership elsewhere, Nasser began to support left-leaning Arab governments. In Yemen, where a

Cairo, the largest city in Africa, was founded in 969. Medieval streets and mosques share its 69 square miles with modern, streamlined buildings, many of them built during Gamal Nasser's presidency.

rebellion against a monarchy was already under way, Nasser sent troops in support of the republicans, only to get bogged down in a seemingly endless war.

Sadat had complete command of the Yemen campaign. Despite his initial enthusiastic assurances to Nasser that it would be a "picnic on the Red Sea," events proved him wrong. The "picnic" turned into a disaster—five years later, with 70,000 troops committed in Yemen, Sadat was blaming the military while Nasser was blaming him. Abysmal though this predicament was, a greater disaster was imminent.

Early in May 1967 Nasser received military intelligence reports which suggested that Israel was about to attack Syria. He mobilized the Egyptian army in the Sinai and ordered that access to the southern Israeli port of Eilat be cut off completely. He also requested the removal of United Nations troops from the border area. On June 5, 1967, while Egypt's defenses were undergoing final inspection by senior officers and general mobilization was still incomplete, squadrons of Israeli

By 1974, Jordan's King Hussein (at left; b. 1927) was able to hold a cordial dialogue with Anwar Sadat, by then president of Egypt. Four years earlier, however, Hussein's attack on the Palestine Liberation Organization (PLO) had severely strained relations between the two countries.

aircraft caught almost the entire Egyptian air force on the ground and wiped it out. Employing recently purchased advanced French warplanes, the Israeli raids had been planned so as to arrive over their various targets at almost exactly the same time. This meant that the Egyptians had no chance to scramble planes from one airfield in response to an attack on another. With 309 out of 340 working aircraft destroyed, Egyptian retaliation was impossible. Encountering only minimal opposition, Israeli ground forces seized all the Sinai Peninsula up to the Suez Canal within just six days. After Syria and Jordan joined the war, Israel also captured the Golan Heights and the west bank of the Jordan river. At least 3,000 Egyptian soldiers died, along with 600 Syrians and 700 Jordanians.

The horror of the situation almost destroyed Nasser physically, leaving him, in Sadat's words, looking like "a living corpse." So devastated was this strong man, this dictator, that he resigned. But popular demonstrations in support of Nasser soon persuaded him to return to power, and, once reinstated, he set about making some necessary changes.

The more conservative Arab governments proved willing to lend Egypt money for the reconstruction of its defenses, but only on the condition that Nasser stop attacking them in his speeches. Nasser, in turn, proceeded to dismiss a number of corrupt officers and began to modernize the army, including in his plans the creation of a special commando force. Rebuilding the shattered Egyptian air force was more of a problem, since the Soviet Union, the one country willing to help in this area, was only prepared to send defensive equipment. The Soviets did, however, send large numbers of technicians, with the result that Soviet military personnel became a familiar sight in Cairo.

At the same time, Nasser faced serious divisions among his own supporters. Leftist military officers, led by Ali Sabri, were convinced that tighter controls on private business and closer ties with the Soviet Union would give Egypt the economic and military advantages it needed. Opposing this group were the right-wing officers and business-men who had grown rich in modern Egypt. They fully intended to protect their positions. Nasser, exhausted and depressed, needed allies who were in neither camp, and found one in Sadat, a man of few strong opinions other than those which Nasser wanted promoted. Much to Sadat's surprise, Nasser made him vice-president in 1969.

The following year, Nasser was pushed to the limit again, this time by conflict among Arabs. In Jordan, where the Palestinian Arab nationalist movement—the Palestine Liberation Organization—had settled, King Hussein came to the conclusion that the organization's civil and military expansion now represented a direct threat to Jordanian sovereignty.

In September 1970 the Jordanian army attacked the PLO, driving it out of the country. This

Shouting "We will take our homeland!" Palestinian Arabs in the Egyptian militia raise their rifles and call for war with Israel. A month later, in June 1967, Egyptian forces were annihilated by the Israelis during what became known as the Six-Day War.

PLO soldiers man an outpost in the Gaza Strip in May 1967. At Nasser's request, United Nations peacekeeping troops had just been withdrawn from the area, which the Israelis were to capture the following month.

event severely damaged the cause of Arab unity. Previously there had been general and constant agreement among all Arab governments, both conservative and socialist, that the restoration of Palestinian rights should be achieved by war against Israel. The Arab world received another shock when Nasser began seriously to consider seeking a peace treaty with Israel. As the leader of the nation that would have to make the greatest contribution in any future conflict with Israel, Nasser was naturally more interested in securing peace than were the other Arab nations. At the same time, he had no wish to see Arab unity undermined.

Faced with this critical situation, Nasser convened an emergency conference, which went so badly that he collapsed shortly after saying his final farewells to the departing Arab diplomats. On September 29, 1970, doctors quietly summoned Sadat to inform him that Nasser was dead.

Nasser had been very much loved throughout the Arab world. His death prompted mourning in every Arab country. Towns and villages held funeral services for the dead leader. In Beirut tens of thousands of people lit bonfires and exploded fireworks in his honor. In Cairo people climbed trees and lampposts to watch the funeral procession go by. The crowd was so thick when it began that it took an hour for the cortege to go the first 100 yards. The coffin was finally moved to an armored car, which then plowed its way through the wailing, chanting crowds.

Stripped of their boots and uniforms, Egyptian prisoners of war are checked by Israeli soldiers in June 1967. Poorly trained and insufficiently prepared for war, the Egyptians were no match for the better-equipped and technologically superior Israeli forces. "They just took off their shoes and ran," said one Israeli officer.

6

"Signal Left, Turn Right"

Sadat, the new president, was greeted with silence, and then laughter. Since he had no reputation other than that of having been Nasser's public relations man, popular opinion of him was not so much low as nonexistent. Other officials had sneeringly referred to him as "Nasser's pet dog," and he found himself the butt of many jokes. In one of these, a Cairo taxi driver, showing his country cousin the sights of the city, stops at a cafe, where the peasant, seeing a picture of Nasser shaking hands with Sadat, asks, "Who is that with our great, blessed leader, Nasser?" The taxi driver, not knowing, but wishing to hide his ignorance, replies, "Oh, that's the cafe owner. "

Another joke ridiculed Sadat's reputation as a shaper of images rather than policy. Sadat leaves the house on his way to parliament, and his chauffeur asks, "Which way, sir?" "Which way did Nasser go?" responds Sadat. "Left, sir." "Then signal left and turn right," replies Sadat.

This is a fairly accurate description of the nature of Sadat's leadership. While he always insisted that he was continuing Nasser's policies,

Leading Egyptian leftist Ali Sabri (behind man in white hat) prepares to cast his ballot in a 1965 election. Sabri's efforts to steer Egypt toward the Soviet camp failed when Sadat appointed him to the vice-presidency—and then simply ignored his recommendations.

When, in 1970, he became Egypt's third president, Anwar Sadat, who had always operated in Nasser's shadow, was virtually unknown both at home and abroad. During the next 11 years, however, he would come to be regarded as a leading statesman.

he actually allowed a wealthy new class to grow and dismantled many of Nasser's populist programs.

Having acquired his prominence precisely because he belonged to neither left nor right, Sadat now had to choose between them and act accordingly. The first challenge to his authority came from the left, from those who dominated Nasser's party, the Arab Socialist Union, now led by Ali Sabri. Sadat responded to this threat by making Ali Sabri vice-president and then proceeding to ignore him, as well as other prominent members of the Arab Socialist Union. When, following Sadat's dismissal of two key ministers, the whole cabinet resigned, hoping thus to bring down the government, Sadat simply accepted their resignations and put his own people in power.

In a further attempt to discredit his opponents Sadat announced that his security officers had discovered secret papers containing evidence of a left-wing plot to overthrow him. He ordered mass arrests and dissolved the Arab Socialist Union. (The impressive ASU headquarters building later housed the Egyptian offices of several major inter-

> *For political matters I must try to give my husband the peace and silence he needs to think and work. Sometimes he asks my opinion, but that does not mean he takes my advice. He does not need advice. He is a leader.*
>
> —JIHAN SADAT

Anwar Sadat's wife Jihan enjoyed the luxuries of high position, but she also worked hard on such projects as the rehabilitation of wounded soldiers and the establishment of rights for women.

national corporations.) To alleviate the increasingly widespread fear that he would become a dictator, Sadat declared the presidency a one-time, six-year term.

Having thus disposed of his opponents, the president set about improving his political image and establishing his own policies. Making use once again of his public relations skills, he began holding "fireside chats" on television, addressing the people of Egypt as "my children," and promoting himself as a family man, as one who had been a child of rural Egypt and was now the father of all Egypt. He also cultivated as luxurious a lifestyle as that of the pharaohs of ancient Egypt, moving his family into a mansion once occupied by King Farouk. Unlike Nasser, who had lived very simply, and during whose era the mansion had been a museum, Sadat sought to live like a king, and succeeded in so doing. He eventually owned ten luxury homes, complete with landscaped gardens and helicopter ports. His wife also was treated as royalty; when Jihan Sadat traveled by airplane, officials would have a red carpet awaiting her arrival.

In addition to securing his position inside Egypt, Sadat had to make definite decisions concerning future foreign policy. The most immediate and important question was the same one that Nasser had faced the day he died—would the Arab nations again wage war on Israel?

In negotiations at the United Nations, Israel was still refusing to set a date for withdrawal from territory it had won in 1967. At the same time, a ceasefire agreement was about to run out, and it had been claimed by Sabri's group that Nasser was secretly preparing for war when he died.

Sadat decided to follow Nasser's last public example. Although Nasser had received no response to his 1970 proposals for peace negotiations, Sadat openly offered Israel a full peace treaty in 1971, on the condition that the disputed territories be returned. He also decided to extend the ceasefire.

Few people favored the position Sadat had adopted. Israel, supported by the United States, rejected the peace offer outright, a move later ex-

> *Egyptian willpower is a collective one, not the monopoly of one person or group.*
> —ANWAR SADAR

Anwar Sadat makes a pilgrimage in 1971 to the holy city of Mecca, the Saudi Arabian birthplace of Muhammad. A devoutly religious man, Sadat disliked having to accept military and economic aid from the officially atheistic communist nations.

plained by Henry Kissinger as due to the fact that America wanted to postpone a settlement until asked to intercede by an Arab state. Sadat's search for peace looked like weakness to the many Egyptians still smarting from the humiliating defeat of 1967.

Aware of the problem, Sadat began to use the threat of war in an attempt to force negotiations and, at the same time, rally his people. Calling 1971 the "Year of Decision," he talked of secret plans, blackouts, and troop mobilization during his regular broadcasts on radio and television. The waiting began to fray people's nerves, since despite this talk of "decision," Sadat still continued to extend the ceasefire. At one point, this lack of decision provoked an Egyptian army captain to lead a convoy into a Cairo square and call for immediate war, claiming that his soldiers were going crazy

U.S. secretary of state Henry Kissinger backed Israel's rejection of Sadat's 1971 peace proposal, but he later played an important role in Mideast peace negotiations.

from waiting.

The "Year of Decision" turned into a year of indecision. At the end of 1971 a joke circulated throughout Cairo which claimed that Sadat, instead of extending the ceasefire one more time, had simply issued a decree extending the year 1971.

As often happens in crisis-ridden countries, popular enthusiasm for war increases as the domestic situation deteriorates. The state of affairs in Egypt had now reached just such a critical point. Unemployment and overcrowding were major problems, and there was little prospect of relief. Workers went on strike. Corruption reached new levels, marked by a wave of arson intended to destroy evidence of scandal. The situation was made more difficult when sectarian fighting broke out between two religious minorities, the Coptic Christians and the fundamentalist Muslims. Students—the hope of the new middle class—also staged demonstrations calling for more freedom of expression.

Sadat had few options. He lacked the real power to clean up corruption, especially since he had alienated his previous supporters on the left, without whose assistance he had almost no chance of successfully challenging the rich and powerful. He made some symbolic gestures, such as granting students the right to travel abroad, but he continued with generally repressive measures, such as censoring the news (to hide the true extent of the problems he faced), passing laws limiting free speech (such as one which made the spreading of rumors a criminal offense), and freely using the police to break up demonstrations.

> *I am for respecting the customs of the people ... not chaining them to a dead past but ... respecting the essential and invisible communities in a nation's life. We would conserve everything that did not impede the real progress of the community.*
> —ANWAR SADAT

Many people were angered by these measures, and in September 1972 hundreds of writers protested censorship. In response, Sadat ordered the arrests of dozens of students, writers, and other professionals. He even closed the universities. He justified his actions by announcing on radio and television that he had prevented a major conspiracy.

One demonstration provoked by these measures gives a good indication of the situation Sadat now faced. The mothers of those arrested gathered in public gardens in Cairo, carrying banners that read, "Our sons for Sinai and not for Egyptian jails." Indeed, the people of Egypt were ready for war.

Sadat, however, was not. Arab disunity combined with Soviet reluctance to give Egypt new weapons made war completely impractical at this point. The Soviets were seeking to establish a more peaceful relationship, called "détente," with the United States, and had undertaken not to provoke war between third parties.

Sadat was not personally sympathetic to the Soviets. As a man of precise religious habits, who prayed five times a day, he found the atheism of the Soviet government disturbing. He might, however, have overlooked it had the Soviets been prepared to give him the weapons he wanted.

Even when a shipment had been promised, Sadat was often forced to negotiate for months over its arrival. One time he even resorted to employing his theatrical skills, dressing up in a Soviet military uniform and sending for the chief Soviet advisor. "Who do you see sitting in front of you?" he asked. "I am Field Marshal Joseph Stalin, that's who!" he yelled. Dressed up as the Soviet Union's most ruthless leader of modern times, he went on to say, "If those spare parts don't get here immediately, I am going to deal with you the way Stalin did." (Stalin had sent many of his political opponents into exile in Siberia, one of the coldest and most inhospitable areas in the entire Soviet Union.)

This particular incident was not only dramatic, but also quite prophetic. When the Soviets simply failed to respond, Sadat called their embassy and gave them two days in which to leave. The Egyptians were generally delighted with Sadat's move, since he had thus demonstrated that Egypt was not afraid to give orders to a superpower. Many people had disliked the presence of Soviet advisors in Cairo in the first place.

It soon became clear that this had been not so much a gesture of independence as a bid for a new allegiance. Sadat really wanted Egypt to be the Arab state most favored by America. To that end he declared that his government was ready to act as

The communist policy goes against our three fundamental principles: national unity; the socialist solution, which includes democracy for the welfare of mankind; and social peace, because they have accepted bloody struggle and claim that it is class struggle which motivates history.

—ANWAR SADAT

an intermediary with other Arab nations on America's behalf. Sadat hoped that this would gain Egypt on-time deliveries of military hardware such as that which Israel received from the Americans. He also hoped thus to secure more economic aid and better terms on major loans.

This combination of gesture and gamble made Sadat suddenly popular in Egypt, though it totally confused the Americans. Henry Kissinger could not understand why Sadat had ordered the Soviets out before asking the United States for anything.

But Sadat was a man of grand gestures and sudden impulses. This time it had paid off, if only in the short run, and he found himself almost as popular in Egypt as if he had declared war.

A desperately poor Cairo family—one of thousands—searches for scraps in a city garbage dump in the early 1970s. Along with political instability at home and abroad, Sadat inherited a nation plagued by poverty and terrible unemployment.

7

War at Last

I will walk to the ends of the earth to keep Egyptian soldiers from getting killed again, if I can still achieve an honorable solution by peaceful means.
—ANWAR SADAT
speaking to members of Egypt's armed forces in 1971

By this time, whenever he talked of war, Sadat gained only the partial attention of the Egyptian people, who regarded such outbursts as instances of Sadat crying wolf. He received even less attention whenever he tried to talk peace, especially when he did so internationally. He had more luck improving relations with conservative Arab governments in 1973. He also tried to impress the Americans with Egypt's willingness to restore relations with Jordan, although he never referred to the Jordanian attack on the PLO, which had been the formal reason for the rift between the two countries.

Sadat also had some fences to mend at home. He pardoned most of the intellectuals he had arrested in 1972, admitting that the conspiracy charges had been quite unfounded. He also insisted that war plans, which always had to be kept secret, might be announced at any time. No one paid any attention.

Then suddenly, on October 6, the Egyptians were victorious in a great battle, the Crossing of the Suez, a superbly well-organized military operation that one Egyptian general referred to as "a magnificent symphony played by tens of thousands of men."

As his nation's armed forces prepared for war during the first nine months of 1973, Sadat talked publicly about the options, military and otherwise, that were available to his government in the area of foreign policy. His ambivalent pronouncements greatly confused the Israelis, and partially explain their lack of preparedness when confronted by Egypt's assault across the Suez Canal that October.

Wearing full military regalia, Anwar Sadat makes a radio address to the Arab world during the Yom Kippur War. The outbreak of hostilities was greeted with wild enthusiasm by the Egyptian people.

Israeli prime minister Golda Meir (in headscarf; 1898–1978) visits an army outpost in the Golan Heights on October 10, 1973, when Israeli troops had just retaken the strategic area four days after its capture by Syrian forces.

The assault took place on Yom Kippur, the holiest day in the Jewish calendar, and caught the Israelis completely off their guard. Before dawn, thousands of commandos crossed the canal in rubber dinghies, armed with portable bazookas and missile launchers. Huge fire hoses sprayed the eastern bank of the canal, demolishing sandbagged strongpoints and clearing a route for tanks. Within hours, Egyptian forces controlled the eastern bank.

Meanwhile, in a coordinated attack, Syrian tanks moved against Israeli forces on the Golan Heights, a disputed area on the border between the two countries. Other Arab states entered the conflict; Iraq and Libya both made significant military contributions.

In Europe the war was widely seen as the result of a breakdown in diplomacy, and due largely to the fact that Israel had failed to return the territory seized in the 1967 war. In the United States the war was considered an unfair attack on an American ally.

In Egypt men of all ages enlisted. Long lines formed at Red Cross centers, as people waited patiently to give blood. But even as the Egyptians were celebrating their victory, the tide of battle turned. The Israelis quickly reorganized, and within four days drove the Syrians not only off the Golan Heights but to within 20 miles of the Syrian capital of Damascus. Having thus successfully countered the immediate threat from Syria, the Israelis were free to turn their attention to the situation at Suez. In a brilliant maneuver on October 16, 200 Israeli soldiers led by General Ariel Sharon sneaked across the canal. After a short but furious fight, they captured the western bank, thus isolating Egyptian forces east of the canal. Sadat's refusal to send reinforcements to the western bank only compounded the disaster.

The Arabs had one more weapon, however, the nature of which was economic, not military. It was provided by a longtime friend of the United States, King Faisal of Saudi Arabia. Faisal had grown frustrated with the lack of American help he himself received, and was appalled by America's seemingly unlimited aid to Israel. He had also become friends with Sadat. On October 17, Saudi Arabia and other Arab oil producers announced that they were commencing a 5% cutback in oil production for all Western backers of Israel. Oil consumption in the United States had already increased by a third between 1969 and 1973, and this latest blow raised fears of oil shortages, throwing the whole country into a panic. People lined up at the pumps to get the last possible gallon into their cars before their local gas station ran out.

In spite of this critical and quite unexpected development, American support for Israel continued. President Nixon immediately asked Congress for emergency funds for Israel's military effort, a

> *Nasser was the symbol of the people's authority. After his departure, the authority of the people can only be guaranteed by constitutional and legal safeguards.*
> —HASANEIN HEIKAL
> Egyptian journalist

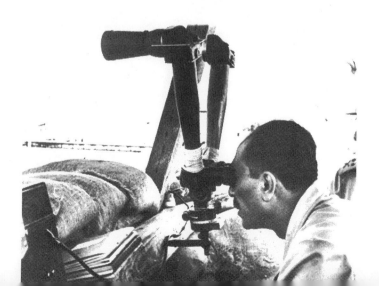

Peering through periscope binoculars in a sandbagged Egyptian bunker, Anwar Sadat checks Israeli positions on the eastern bank of the Suez Canal in 1971. Egypt's surprise attack on the canal two years later was successful, but the wider campaign that it preceded failed.

Four years after the Yom Kippur War, Egyptian air force planes roar through the skies over Cairo during a military parade that included U.S. transport planes, French and Soviet jet fighters, and British helicopters.

request that provoked Faisal into ordering further cutbacks in Saudi oil production.

The war had moved to a new level, with serious implications for the rest of the world. Even the Soviet Union was worried by the possibility of a Mideast war escalating to a point where the superpowers became involved. Sadat, who could neither win nor quit, asked the Russians to sponsor a ceasefire resolution in the United Nations, which they did. But the Israelis kept on fighting, cutting off the road to Suez and capturing 45,000 Egyptian

General Moshe Dayan (wearing eyepatch; 1915–1981), Israel's defense minister and a hero of the Six-Day War of 1967, discusses tactics with his officers on the second day of the Yom Kippur War.

soldiers and 250 tanks. Finally, a United Nations emergency force arrived to supervise a ceasefire.

In Egypt and other Arab countries, the ceasefire was as unpopular as the war had been popular. At Suez, for example, the townspeople refused at first to obey orders to surrender. But Sadat had no intention of resuming hostilities. Even so, the war came to be seen in Egypt and other Arab countries as a partial victory, because the Crossing had been decisive proof of Egyptian courage and skill.

Finally, Sadat had established by war what he could not by talking peace: he had made it necessary for the United States to take an interest in negotiations, and had also made clear his terms for such negotiations, namely, the return of Egyptian territory.

The Yom Kippur War clarified the issues. Israel wanted the Arab world to recognize it and live in peace with it, while the Arab world wanted Israel to pull back to its 1948 boundaries. Egypt in particular wanted the Gaza Strip and the Sinai returned, while the Arabs in general wanted Jerusalem made an international city again and the need of Palestinian Arabs for their own state acknowledged by Israel.

Listen, my son... I called for you today in order to ask you one question, and I want to hear from you a clear and definite answer. Tell me, my son, is the air force ready for battle or not? Think before you give me an answer....
We have been struck twice and if the air force is struck for the third time, that would be the end of us.
—ANWAR SADAT
speaking to Egyptian air force commander Hosni Mubarak on September 28, 1973

8

The War at Home

October 6, 1973, was a day of glory for Sadat, but within two weeks he faced the same problems that had dogged him prior to the military success of the first round of fighting at Suez. Egypt had gone to war with its economy already crippled by long-term loss of revenues from both the Suez Canal and the Sinai oil fields. Now it found itself even deeper in debt due to the expenses of the fighting. The situation was made worse by the fact that Sadat had few places to look for help. Although the Soviet Union remained the major purchaser of Egyptian goods, Sadat's expulsion of Soviet advisors and diplomats had caused the Soviet Union to terminate direct aid to Egypt. His eager acceptance of a ceasefire had angered the other Arab countries, and he had failed to strike up a working relationship with the Americans.

In the immediate aftermath of the 1973 war, Sadat needed friends desperately, a state of affairs reflected in his two most important new policies. On the home front, economic development programs went into effect, with particular emphasis on encouraging private investment. Egyptian foreign policy began to seek closer ties with the United States.

Sadat's new economic policy was an attempt to change direction from the Nasser era, when the government had run many of the businesses. But he had to do it without angering the people who

I never before believed in the role of the individual in history, but the hero, Anwar Sadat, is beyond my comprehension.
—YOUSSEF IDRIS
Egyptian journalist

A United Nations Food and Agricultural Organization representative demonstrates the use of a well in an impoverished Egyptian village. In the nation's primitive rural areas, pure water was often a luxury.

Farmers buy and sell livestock and produce at a typical Egyptian market. Following Sadat's 1975 farm legislation, many peasants were forced to leave their land and seek work in the overcrowded cities.

had benefited from those programs—the corrupt officials who had sabotaged the nationalized industries, and the poor, who had become largely dependent on government social welfare. He announced his great plan in October 1974, calling it *al-Infitah*, or "the Opening." It was intended to be the moral equivalent of the Crossing, an economic program as daring as the lightning raid across the Suez Canal, aimed at opening up the Egyptian economy to more private investment both from home and from overseas.

Sadat's formula was simple. He wanted to combine foreign money, especially Arab oil money, with modern technology and cheap Egyptian labor and markets, hoping thereby to promote economic growth. He proposed to establish "free trade zones" in major Egyptian cities. Here goods could be imported and exported without being taxed. He wanted to expand tourism and develop the Sinai. He also hoped that improved relations with other Arab oil-producing nations (such as Saudi Arabia, Qatar, and Kuwait) would better guarantee the jobs of the thousands of Egyptians already employed there. Many working-class Egyptian families depended on money earned abroad.

Sadat tried to encourage foreign investors by offering them a variety of incentives. He promised to tax and to regulate new investment lightly if at

Sadat (at center) enjoyed spending time with his family. Here, he is accompanied by (from the left) his son-in-law Abdel Ghaffar, daughters Lobna and Jihan, wife Jihan, daughter Noha, and son-in-law Hassan Marei.

An Egyptian perches high on a wall overlooking one of the three gigantic pyramids at Giza. Sadat's plan to increase tourism in the area by authorizing the construction of a Western-style leisure complex on this historic site was abandoned after it met widespread opposition.

all. He guaranteed that Egyptian labor would remain cheap and docile. Also included in the package were assurances that Egypt would make investments of its own in the form of road repairs, improved electrical systems, and equipment modernization.

The idea itself, while spectacular, proved overly ambitious. The public sector, originally created through Nasser's government programs, and staffed by the increasing numbers of young college graduates, was now a huge bureaucracy. Sadat would only have made more enemies in attempting to reduce it. Egypt had little money in the treasury with which to make improvements, and Sadat was in no position to demand much more from the poor, who had no more to give.

It is not surprising that the Opening failed to bring new hope to the majority of the people. It actually increased the luxurious habits of the rich and led to even greater corruption.

Tourism did increase following Sadat's announcement. Hotels that in the Nasser era had catered to a handful of tired diplomats and bored Soviet advisors were now remodeled and came to be fully occupied by international business consultants and bankers, all trying to work out how to take advantage of Sadat's offers. For breakfast, they could have mineral water from Italy, butter from France, grapefruit juice from Florida, and croissants from Egypt. Nightclubs became even more glamorous, and Arabs looking into investment opportunities indulged themselves in Cairo's nightlife. There were plans for the construction of a leisure complex near the Pyramids, in anticipation of large-scale tourism. This "Egyptian Disneyland" was never built, however, due to public protest. There was even a proposal for a $400 million project to create a "Palm Springs on the Nile," a huge resort catering to the jet set.

At first, the prospects were encouraging. The shah of Iran committed $700 million of his nation's money. West Germany provided another $500 million, and Japanese investors put up around $100 million. In every area of business, from carpet weaving to electronics assembly, international partnerships were eagerly promoted.

By the time the dust settled on the dealing, however, it became apparent that Sadat's gamble

A narrow Cairo street is choked with shopkeepers, old-fashioned carts, modern automobiles, peddlers, and an endless stream of people. Already overpopulated, Cairo's situation grew increasingly desperate after 1975 when Sadat's new farm laws drove thousands of dispossessed peasants to seek work in the city.

Cairo's Heliopolis Hotel was typical of the opulent amenities enjoyed by Egypt's tiny upper class and wealthy foreigners.

had failed. Very little of the new money actually ended up in industry. For one thing, foreigners found the Egyptian bureaucracy too confusing. One American called it "like pushing string" to get something done. Another major problem was that Egypt just did not have the facilities that the new industries needed for efficient operation. The ports were old-fashioned, Cairo's sewage system was always breaking down, the streets were full of potholes, and the air in the cities was polluted.

The new foreign money was used instead to finance construction and real estate investment which offered more immediate profits. The shacks and hovels of the poor quickly disappeared as luxury apartment and office buildings shot up all over the big cities. This caused many urban poor to move back onto the farmland that they had originally left because it could no longer support them.

Imported goods are unloaded at the bustling docks of Alexandria, Egypt's second-largest city. In 1974 Sadat introduced his *al-Infitah* program, which called for, among other innovations, the establishment of "free trade zones," where no taxes would be imposed on foreign merchandise.

Only the circumstances of their poverty had changed.

Among those who were snapping up the new luxury accommodations were a number of people making money semilegally: smugglers operating out of the new free trade zones, and public officials selling government-subsidized goods to dealers on the open market.

The greatest changes resulting from the Opening were to be found in farming. Reversing policies established in Nasser's era, Sadat tried to turn farming over to "the free market," and the hapless peasants with it. In 1975 a new law doubled rents, raised the permitted size of farms, and once again deregulated the sale of land. This not only took away the peasants' security, but also resulted in many of them losing the little land they had.

Sadat also encouraged the growing of commercial crops for the private market, causing food prices to soar. Both the commercial growers and the traditional peasant farmers stopped growing basic crops such as wheat, thus forcing Egypt to increase vastly its imports of basic foodstuffs. Peasants, many now landless, began migrating to the city, swelling the population of Cairo.

In the midst of this economic and social confusion, people were increasingly uncertain as to just whom Sadat represented. Though born a peasant, he no longer seemed to have their interests at heart, any more than he did those of the urban poor. He was a product of government schools, but his economic programs failed to create jobs for college graduates. He seemed committed to furthering the fortunes of his own cronies, men such as Osman Ahmad Osman, a rich contractor known as the "Cement King." Osman had helped build the Aswan High Dam and now became an investor in many of the projects established under the auspices of the Opening.

Osman and his kind were the people who bought the expensive liquor, paraded the streets of Cairo in their Peugeots and Mercedes, and packed the nightclubs. They were among the elite 10% of the population who accounted for 60% of all the money spent in Egypt. They maintained a great distance between themselves and the majority of the people. One professional told an American journalist that he found it impossible to hold a conversation even with his own chauffeur, saying, "I feel like a foreigner when I'm with the Egyptian lower class."

Much more dangerous politically was the dissatisfaction of the middle class, who had seen the rich getting richer while they themselves had increasing trouble finding jobs. They were the so-

In every soldier who fell in the Arab-Israeli War of 1973 there is a son and a part of our soul. . . . Wars know no real victor, no real vanquished . . . the price is enormous and painful. It is the sacrifice of thousands of young people, the mourning and grief in the hearts of the mothers, the wives, the fathers.
—JIHAN SADAT
during an interview with *The Times* of London in March 1974

Like Cairo, Alexandria teems with people, many of them underfed, unemployed, and crowded into inadequate housing. Successive Egyptian governments, Sadat's included, recognized that such conditions tended to breed generations of potential revolutionaries.

called "invisible" Egyptians, people who had hoped that war would change their lives and that the workings of the free market would change their economic circumstances.

During the 1973 war, a young soldier's diary was published after his death. It told a story with which many Egyptians were able to identify. He was the son of peasants who had been thrown off the land and forced to move to a slum in Alexandria. There his father had become a movie house doorman and his mother a factory worker. He had lived with the other seven members of his family in a hovel 13 feet square, sharing a toilet with six other families. Even though he had spent four years in the army and had earned a college degree, he could find no employment. "We live in poverty, without hope," he wrote. "We are mere dogs and slaves."

When war broke out, he had become charged with energy and optimism. "Perhaps there will be some purpose to my life now," he wrote. But the Israelis captured the young marine and his comrades and executed them when they tried to escape. As he awaited death, he made a list of the things he loved most in life. Among them were the music of Mozart, the Koran, and films like *Cabaret*.

It was people like this officer, Muhammad Nadda, who looked to Anwar Sadat for the answers to life-and-death questions. Unfortunately, there were no easy answers, as became even clearer when rioting erupted in 1977.

There had been previous demonstrations and strikes. On New Year's Day, 1975, while parading past hotels where wealthy couples had just spent, for one evening's entertainment, the amount of money a worker earned in a whole year, Cairo's poor had shouted, "O Hero of the Crossing, where is our breakfast?" Three months later strikes had broken out at textile mills. Angry workers who lived on a diet of bread and beans broke into their bosses' homes and they discovered cases of whiskey and frozen turkeys.

Sadat made a few feeble attempts to placate the poor, lowering basic food prices and ordering some arrests on charges of corruption. He also

Students assembled in downtown Cairo's Liberation Square prepare to conduct a mass demonstration against the government. Riots paralyzed much of Egypt in 1977.

On October 10, 1975, Israel officially returns to Egyptian control the western Sinai oilfields, seized during the Yom Kippur War two years earlier.

increased taxes on luxuries such as casino gambling and negotiated for emergency loans from foreign countries, including Arab states.

The one bank from which Sadat failed to extract a loan was the one with the most money: the International Monetary Fund. The IMF refused to lend to Egypt until Sadat promised to reduce government spending on the Egyptian poor. The IMF thought the government too generous with scarce funds, and wanted proof that Egypt would make the sacrifices necessary to guarantee repayment of the loans. Finally, in 1977, Sadat took the only course open to him. He cut the subsidies on basic food items such as bread and beans.

Immediately, protest demonstrations were staged, and riots soon followed. For 36 hours the major cities of Egypt were in turmoil. Some of the most exclusive boutiques and nightclubs were looted and suburban trains were attacked. People tore up the rails because they were angry about conditions on the train system—so badly run and overcrowded that nearly every week someone died trying to get to work. As the violence continued, Egypt appeared to be on the brink of civil war.

Sadat immediately issued harsh emergency decrees curtailing civil rights. He blamed the riots on a few communists and his old enemy, Ali Sabri. Once more he moved against his political opponents, ordering mass arrests. These were difficult and dangerous times for Anwar Sadat.

> *I have always mistrusted theories and purely rational systems. I believe in the power of concrete facts, and the realities of history and experience. My political ideas grew out of my personal experience of oppression, not out of abstract notions.*
> —ANWAR SADAT

9

Performing for Peace

In 1973 Sadat's initial triumph in the war with Israel seemed to have won him international prestige, but the fruits of this partial success eluded him. He now needed peace desperately, and came to believe, almost mystically, that peace with Israel would bring prosperity. War had gained him little more than heavier debts.

Sadat's outstanding skill in politics had been in a kind of advertising — call it what you wish: propaganda, public relations, information management. It involved theatrics, persuasion, and timing. Sadat now set about employing these skills so as to achieve something unprecedented in the Arab world: to persuade American officials to view Egypt in much the same way they did Israel. Few Americans had ever shown much interest in either Arab or Muslim culture and history, while they thought of Israel as an essentially Western nation situated in the Middle East. America, as a superpower that supported Israel, was extremely important to Sadat's efforts.

There were two other major considerations: Israel and the Arab countries. Israel and Egypt had long viewed each other with much suspicion and hostility. One Israeli journalist, Amos Elon, put it well. "For years we have lived apart from each other. . . . Behind every Israeli soldier, Egyptians saw a French Foreign Legionnaire or an English colonialist. Behind every Egyptian soldier, Israelis

> *Sadat has stimulated an intense thirst for freedom which he will be bound in some measure to satisfy. . . . I have known Egypt for 15 years, and I have never heard Egyptians express themselves as openly as they do now.*
> —EDWARD SHEEHAN
> American journalist, writing in 1971

Portraits of Richard Nixon and Anwar Sadat stand in readiness along the route from the Cairo airport to welcome the visiting American president in 1974.

Henry Kissinger (at left) meets with Saudi Arabia's King Faisal (1905–1975) to discuss the Arab oil embargo. Faisal, as a spokesman for the Arab oil-producing nations, said Arab oil exports would continue to dwindle until Israel changed its attitude toward the demands of the Palestinian Arabs.

saw an SS man bent on genocide. We have lived for years in a world of demons and devils." The Israelis also understood that the United States was their strongest defensive support, and were careful to protect their image as America's best friend in the Middle East.

The second obstacle confronting Sadat was the Arab unity that Nasser had so promoted and developed. The only two things upon which most Arab leaders agreed were hostility to Israel and support for the Palestinian Arabs. Any attempt by one Arab state to negotiate a separate peace with Israel might well invalidate that state's claim to represent Arab interests, alienate the other states, and damage the united front. This held especially true for Egypt, the most prominent of the Arab states.

Making Americans sympathetic to Egypt without appearing to give in to Israel and thereby losing the support of other Arab nations was the toughest assignment Sadat had ever set himself. He was forced to try it or risk losing his power at home. Still, it took courage to attempt something so bold that no one had ever tried it.

For reasons readily apparent at every gas pump in the United States, the events of 1973 made Americans eager to improve relations with the Arab countries. The oil embargo continued to create panic. And King Faisal of Saudi Arabia warned Henry Kissinger that he intended to go on cutting production until America had put sufficient pressure on the Israeli government to force it to return the occupied territories and recognize Palestinian Arab rights.

Kissinger also saw the Middle East as an issue that might be used to improve the image of President Nixon, whose political fortunes were fast declining due to the Watergate scandal. (His election campaign workers had been discovered stealing campaign documents from their rivals, and

The Suez Canal, which had been in constant use since first opening in 1869, was closed by the Egyptian government upon the outbreak of the Six-Day War of 1967. Although it was considered a risky act, Sadat reopened the canal in 1975 "for the sake," he said, "of peace."

Aboard the train carrying them from Cairo to Alexandria in 1974, Richard Nixon (extending his arm in salute) and a beaming Anwar Sadat greet some of the thousands of wellwishers who lined the way.

Nixon's part in the subsequent coverup was becoming increasingly evident.)

Kissinger offered to help in what he called "step by step" diplomacy, which meant not only taking up issues one by one, but also striking individual deals between different Arab nations and Israel. In December 1973 the United States helped set up a United Nations conference, at which Israel agreed to pull back from the eastern bank of the Suez Canal. Kissinger then met with officials in Israel and Syria for negotiations which resulted in the two countries signing an agreement, in May 1974, under the terms of which Israel was not required to withdraw any further from occupied territory.

From the Arab viewpoint, this was hardly an impressive beginning. Although the embargo was lifted, Arab leaders not only grumbled to Sadat about the treaties , but also to each other about Sadat. Still, this was the first sign Sadat had of American interest in Egypt. He was further delighted when, in June 1974, President Richard Nixon visited Egypt, although many people suspected that Nixon was really using the visit solely to divert attention from his growing domestic scandal.

Sadat, however, was happy to make the most of the occasion. He made sure that there were huge crowds to greet Nixon. He even sent messages to government offices about the proper clothing to be worn by public employees, for whom the day had been declared a holiday. He proudly escorted Nixon around the Pyramids, and lavished gifts on him (as he would later on President Carter), even going so far as to present him with precious antiquities from Cairo's museums.

The Americans tried to convince Israel to negotiate with Egypt over withdrawal from the Sinai. This was difficult, especially since many Israelis felt that giving up any gains made in war would set a bad example and endanger their future security.

Sadat, meanwhile, continued to take risks. In June 1975, even though the Israelis were still within shooting distance, he reopened the Suez

A solemn Anwar Sadat (at center) arrives in Israel on November 21, 1977. Greeting the Egyptian president on his historic visit is Israeli prime minister Menachem Begin (left).

Canal. It had been closed since 1967, costing Egypt hundreds of millions of dollars in lost revenues. (The canal, which is one of four major sources of government income, put $600 million into Egypt's treasury in 1980 alone.)

Finally, in September 1975 Israel agreed to leave the Sinai Peninsula—for a price. Kissinger, now representing the administration of Gerald Ford, had to promise that the United States would send up-to-date military equipment to Israel. He also had to give assurances that America would not recognize or negotiate with the PLO until that organization recognized Israel. For his part, Sadat had to promise that Egypt would remain neutral if Israel and Syria went to war. Since he had thus made a separate deal with Israel, however indi-

Former Israeli prime minister Golda Meir and Egyptian president Anwar Sadat exchange smiles and a warm handshake as they meet in the Knesset building during Sadat's 1977 visit to Israel.

rectly, Arab leaders became even more distrustful of Sadat.

When, in 1977, riots broke out and civil war threatened, everyone watched Egypt closely. Fearing possible chaos, some Arab nations sent Egypt emergency funds. The United States sent $200 million (which had previously been intended for other Egyptian needs such as the payment for short-term debts) and the IMF relaxed some of its rules in order to reduce the pressure under which the Egyptian government found itself.

Sadat, realizing that these were only temporary measures, decided to take an all-or-nothing gamble. He announced that he would go anywhere to make peace, even into the Knesset, the Israeli parliament. He made it sound like the biblical story of Daniel going into the lion's den.

Sadat's declarations created considerable confusion in Egypt. His own government-controlled newspapers expressed doubts; the Israelis, suspicion. The new prime minister in Israel was Menachem Begin, a conservative who, like Sadat,

Sadat addresses members of the Israeli delegation that, headed by Prime Minister Begin, visited Egypt in December 1977. Seated next to Sadat is Vice-President Hosni Mubarak (b. 1929), who succeeded Sadat as Egypt's president.

had been an underground freedom fighter in his youth. The two men had an intense dislike for each other.

The United States, however, approved of Sadat's idea. American diplomats were nervous about Begin, whose policies seemed more uncompromising than was perhaps desirable in a situation where a real breakthrough was essential. When Begin sent Sadat a formal invitation to visit the Knesset, President Carter held a prayer meeting for peace.

Sadat went to Jerusalem in November 1977, thus becoming the first Egyptian leader to do so since Cleopatra had ventured there 2,000 years earlier to discuss territorial disputes with the Roman official Herod.

His visit proved the importance of dramatic gestures in modern politics. Everywhere his decision caused tumult. Posters appeared in Cairo, showing Sadat wearing a stars-and-stripes hat and an eyepatch (a reference to the Israeli defense minister, Moshe Dayan). In Syria the government declared official mourning. In Israel people wore T-shirts with Sadat's and Begin's faces on them, bearing the slogan "All You Need Is Love."

When Sadat and Begin spoke in the Knesset, it became apparent that real progress would require more than mere gestures. Sadat insisted that Israel leave the occupied territories, saying it was vital that the Israelis understand "the Palestinian people's determination to establish once again a state on their land." Begin—never a man to mince words—replied sharply. "We did not take a foreign country," he told Sadat. "We came back to our homeland." He said nothing about the Palestinian Arabs.

Sadat returned home claiming a victory. In one way he was justified, since although nothing had changed between Egypt and Israel, Westerners now saw Sadat as a world leader, a statesman committed to the cause of peace. As one skilled in public relations, Sadat was perfectly aware of the effect of his newfound stance. So great was the attention he paid to the media that an American

All Egyptians—Muslims and Copts—have for generations taken part in our national battles for liberation and reconstruction.... Plotters from outside our land do not know the nature of this people and the strength of their faith in God.

—ANWAR SADAT

speaking in 1977, in the aftermath of Muslim fundamentalist attacks on Coptic churches and communities

TV producer told Sadat's press aides, "You sure have a great president here. He knows the deadlines for every news show in the States." A month later *Time* magazine named Sadat its "Man of the Year."

Older politicians found this television diplomacy shocking. Israeli leader Golda Meir considered Begin and Sadat little better than showmen. "Never mind the Nobel Peace Prize," she said. "Give them both Oscars."

Henry Kissinger, however, was very much impressed, and no longer thought of Sadat as a clown. He wrote in *Time* magazine, "The very audacity of Sadat's act, like the artificial mountains which are the Pyramids, dwarfs the small calculations of the recent past." Kissinger was not the only American who changed his mind about the Egyptian leader. Opinion polls showed that public sympathy for Israel fell 13% in 1977.

Egyptian and Israeli delegations meet to discuss the possibility of reaching tentative agreement on peace terms in Ismailia, Egypt, in late 1977. Among the Egyptians on the left are Sadat (smoking a pipe) and (next to him, partly hidden) Mubarak. The Israeli contingent includes Begin (in dark-rimmed glasses) and (wearing an eyepatch) Moshe Dayan.

10

Camp David

Like many Americans, President Carter had never given much thought to the Arab world. In his autobiography, he recalled the beginnings of his role in the peace process. In a world where American interests were opposed to those of the Soviet Union, "Israel was a strategic asset to the United States," he wrote. "I had no strong feelings about the Arab countries. I had never visited one and knew no Arab leaders." Carter, a religious man, wanted to help bring about peace in the Middle East, and accordingly invited Begin and Sadat to visit the United States separately for discussions.

When Sadat visited, Carter was very impressed with the Egyptian leader's dignified bearing and his offers of friendship, Carter also came to respect Sadat's precise habits of prayer, rest, and cautious diet. He always ate in private during breaks from the negotiations, went to sleep early, and took an hour's walk in the middle of the day. Sadat's concern for his personal health was particularly pronounced when he was traveling. On his first visit to Camp David, after walking the few hundred yards from the helicopter to his cabin in the cool February air, Sadat became so worried about catching a cold that he went straight to bed. At home, he was used to traveling even short distances by air.

Each step I have taken over the years has been for the good of Egypt, and has been designed to serve the cause of right, liberty, and peace.
—ANWAR SADAT
writing in 1979

Taking a break from their 1978 conference with Israeli prime minister Menachem Begin, Anwar Sadat (at left) and Jimmy Carter set out for a stroll at Camp David, the U.S. president's country retreat.

Anwar Sadat (left) joins Jimmy Carter at the White House before their 1977 discussion about Mideast peace. The two leaders quickly became friends. "I am dealing with a man," said Sadat, "impelled by the power of religious faith—a farmer, like me."

Anwar Sadat waves from his limousine (at right) as a jubilant crowd cheers and throws flowers to celebrate his return from the United States in 1978.

Carter then invited Begin and Sadat to visit Camp David together in September 1978. Both accepted, but the talks went slowly.

Neither side had looked forward to making concessions of any kind, and on several occasions it seemed that the conference might collapse altogether. Finally, Begin put aside his personal feelings regarding Israeli withdrawal from the occupied territories and discontinuation of settlement in those areas. He announced that he was willing to discuss returning the Sinai, but not the other territories, for which the most he would consider was autonomous status. (Autonomy is the right to self-government, but without independence.) Begin also agreed to submit these issues for open debate in the Israeli parliament. Finally, on the 13th day of the conference, the three leaders emerged from their conference, and Carter was able to announce rough drafts on two agreements. One was a separate peace treaty between Israel and Egypt, the other a "framework for peace in the Middle East," a document intended to pave the way for future step-by-step peace negotiations. The documents were not signed but at least a beginning had been made.

The main problem now facing everybody with a stake in the debate was that the Camp David agreements had extracted few substantial concessions from either side. Begin and his advisors had agreed to give up the Sinai but failed to set a time limit for withdrawal. They wanted to retain control of the Gaza Strip, the Golan Heights, and the area on the Israel-Jordan border known as the West Bank. Only autonomy was suggested for the West Bank, and Israel wanted no changes in the status of Jerusalem.

In the West, however, the general reaction was joyful. Jimmy Carter's popularity in the polls

Jimmy Carter applauds as two old enemies—Anwar Sadat (his back to the camera) and Menachem Begin— embrace in the East Room of the White House. The emotional scene took place following the conclusion of the conference between the three leaders at Camp David in 1978.

Members of a Cairo lawyers' association express their opposition to Sadat's peace overtures to Israel by burning an Israeli flag in 1980. The banner reads: "Egypt is an integral part of the Arab nation."

rose 17%. For their historic efforts, Begin and Sadat were honored by being named joint recipients of the Nobel Peace Prize.

While Begin went to collect the award, Sadat stayed home, partly because the agreements had not been signed, and partly because of the rising tide of resentment he faced from the other Arab states, who were furious about Egypt's separate peace and its terms. Even Saudi Arabia, a staunch ally of the United States, refused to accept the accords.

In November 1978 the Arab nations met in an attempt to reach a decision concerning Egypt. Not wishing their united front to appear any more fragile than it already was, they offered Sadat a deal. They agreed to pay him 2.5 billion Egyptian pounds a year on the condition that he refuse to sign the accords. Although Egypt could certainly have used the money for economic and defensive purposes, Sadat knew a bribe when he saw one. He felt the Arab states were hardly helping the cause of peace by seeking a guarantee that Egypt would remain available for involvement in any future conflict. He had no intention of furthering Egyptian prosperity by promising his allies an unlimited supply of Egyptian blood. Indeed, Egypt would always have to be the first to fight and, judging by past performance, would suffer the most casualties. He publicly rejected the Arab offer. Sadat hoped eventually to receive even more money from the United States—up to $15 billion.

Meanwhile, the Israeli government rejected Carter's proposals for final peace treaty terms. Carter responded by visiting both Egypt and Israel for further discussions. Sadat, when asked to make more concessions, agreed not to ask Israel when the occupied territories might gain autonomy. When even this was unacceptable to Begin, it began to look as if the whole deal was off. "We have gone as far as we can in putting forward suggested compromise language," wrote Carter in his diary in March 1979, "with practically no constructive response from Israel." Carter then asked Begin bluntly if he really did want a peace treaty. Begin assured

After months of complex negotiations, Jimmy Carter (seated at center) presides over the signing of the Israeli-Egyptian peace treaty on March 26, 1979. At left is Anwar Sadat, and seated at right is Menachem Begin.

him that he did. Carter then worked out a new deal with the Israelis, who were particularly worried about meeting their energy requirements. Under the terms of the new arrangement Israel would relinquish the Sinai oil fields and Egypt would be required to assume the role of a major supplier. To reassure the Israelis further, the United States guaranteed Israel's oil supplies for the next 15 years should Jerusalem at any time find itself without other sources of supply.

On March 26, 1979, Sadat, Begin, and Carter met on the White House lawn and signed the treaty.

In Israel some people protested loudly at the loss of the Sinai, and a number of settlers refused to consider moving. Others, encouraged by the prospect of peace, made plans to tour the Pyramids or go to Egypt on business. In Egypt the prospect of peace was received with widespread popular enthusiasm. When Sadat arrived back in Cairo, his airplane was met by a crowd of 2 million people, all singing, clapping, and dancing.

It seemed like the dawn of a new era in Egypt. A new national anthem was written, a gentle tune with a folk song influence, quite different from the previous, more military-sounding one. Not everyone was singing along, however. The agreement met with the disapproval of many important Egyptian politicians, one of whom, a former government minister, called it "peace by circus." Another official, who had been a member of the original Free Officers movement, was worried that it would make Egypt "a springboard for a Jewish empire," and that "the true masters of the Sinai will be the Americans." Yet another called the accord outright "surrender," while the Muslim fundamentalists considered Sadat to have betrayed a sacred trust.

Not even Sadat's substantial media skills could hide one important aspect of the Camp David accords: Egypt had acted alone. In response the Arab nations, meeting again, expelled Egypt from both the Arab League and OPEC (Organization of Petroleum Exporting Countries), and cut off all official aid. Saudi Arabia canceled its offer of fighter aircraft.

Sadat now found himself in a position where not only was he considered to have given in to Israel, but he had also lost the support of the Arab world. Possible American generosity was his last hope, and this began to look very uncertain when, in 1980, President Carter failed in his bid for reelection.

There is no doubt that the initial Arab successes in the Arab-Israeli War of 1973 satisfied their feelings of national honor, and facilitated Sadat's ability to develop a dialogue between the two sides, ultimately reaching a peace treaty.

—CHAIM HERZOG
president of Israel

After 15 years of occupation, Israelis lower their flag during the April 25, 1982, ceremony that completed the return of the bitterly contested Sinai Peninsula to Egypt. It was a moment Sadat would have appreciated, but he did not live to see it.

11

Peace at Any Price

Sadat tried to make the most of his reputation as an Arab leader whom Western nations could trust, even inviting the United States to set up military bases in Egypt. He also made the potentially dangerous decision to give refuge to the shah of Iran, who had been overthrown by a Muslim fundamentalist revolution and was now shunned throughout the Arab world. Sadat gave the shah a lavish funeral, which made him even more unpopular with the fundamentalists. Egypt also played "policeman" for American interests, backing the opposition to Libya's leader, Muammar Qaddafi (whom United States officials distrusted), and supporting the pro-Western opponents of the government in Chad. Egypt also sold weapons to Somalia, allowed arms to be smuggled into Eritrea, and provided military aid to the Moroccan government, which was fighting separatist rebels in the Sahara desert. All of these governments were backed by the United States.

In return Sadat received more American help for Egypt than ever before. The United States began delivering arms to Egypt on the same easy credit terms as were allowed to Israel. In March 1979 Carter had sent $1.5 billion in arms to Egypt, and later on sent $3 billion more, along with American advisors. The United States embassy, which in 1973 had been staffed by only six people, came

> *The Middle East has, thanks to President Sadat's initiative, undergone a revolution.... Israel has a peaceful border with Egypt.*
> —CHAIM HERZOG
> president of Israel

Ronald Reagan (b. 1911), with Anwar Sadat at his side, listens to the national anthem during a ceremony welcoming the Egyptian leader to Washington, D.C., in 1981. Reagan told Sadat that his administration hoped to enlarge on the "achievements of Camp David."

Anwar Sadat, his uniform resplendent with military decorations, watches an Egyptian air force display at the parade marking the eighth anniversary of the Yom Kippur War. He was shot moments after this photograph was made.

to employ hundreds, and was moved to a new, 17-story building.

Egypt's national debt, however, continued to mount. Inflation was eating away at people's salaries, and the population continued to grow rapidly, with 1,000 more people moving to Cairo every day.

In 1980 bread shortages afflicted the country. Sadat immediately tried some temporary measures. He raised government salaries and made token cuts in the prices of some foods. Early in 1981 he arranged a solution with more lasting consequences. Meeting with Western bankers, he agreed to mortgage revenues from the Suez Canal and the Sinai oil fields in return for loans.

Libyan leader Muammar Qaddafi (b. 1942), proposed political union between his country and Egypt in 1972. Sadat, however, became increasingly uncomfortable with Qaddafi's uncompromising ambition to destroy Israel, and by 1974 Egypt had joined the United States in denouncing the militant Libyan head of state.

Anwar Sadat visits the ailing shah of Iran, Muhammad Reza Pahlavi (1919–1980), in a Cairo hospital room shortly before the shah's death. Sadat's hospitality to the deposed ruler infuriated his Arab neighbors.

An American army unit equipped with armored personnel carriers prepares for joint exercises with Egyptian troops at a desert base near Cairo in 1981. The Reagan administration continued Jimmy Carter's policy of providing Egypt with military aid.

Sadat also faced political unrest. In May 1978 he had issued a decree giving himself the right to exclude from public life anyone he considered suspicious. A referendum had approved the measure, but most people had failed to cooperate with it. Sadat's political problems were not to be easily concealed. Increasingly, Muslim fundamentalists protested the fact that his rule was allied with the West both politically and socially. The Western social influence was especially obvious when Sadat

A priest outside one of Cairo's Coptic Christian churches. As the influence of the Muslim fundamentalists expanded during the late 1970s, violent acts against the Copts increased. By late 1980, six Coptic churches had been bombed by terrorists.

An Egyptian soldier lofts his Soviet-made rocket launcher as he approaches his American counterparts during joint maneuvers in Egypt in 1981. Once the recipient of vast amounts of Soviet aid, Egypt became increasingly dependent on the United States during the Sadat era.

hosted parties for the jet set.

In 1980 Sadat finally woke up to the extent of the threat posed to his supremacy by fundamentalists. He hurriedly approved legislation that came to be known as the "Law of Shame," which made it illegal to challenge "popular, religious, moral, or national values" in public. Censorship was increased, and a special court was set up to judge crimes within the scope of the new law. At the same time, Sadat made Islamic law, the Shari'a, the basis for all new legislation. He also made himself president for life.

Hosni Mubarak, the commander-in-chief of the Egyptian air force, was 52 years old when he became Egypt's fourth president. A former bomber pilot, Mubarak supervised air operations against Israel during the Yom Kippur War.

In mid-1981, rioting broke out in Cairo between Christian Copts and Muslim fundamentalists. Sadat used the situation as an opportunity to arrest 1,500 of his opponents, including many Muslim fundamentalists. He also made himself his own prime minister.

Sadat was gambling desperately for control, and on October 6, 1981, he lost. It was fundamentalists in the military who pulled up in the jeep and shot him. The 24 defendants expressed no regrets at their trial, since, as their attorney argued, they believed that Sadat had betrayed Muslim law by allowing an atmosphere of terror in the country.

Sadat's vice-president, Hosni Mubarak, escaped unscathed from the assassination, but not from the problems Sadat left behind. He assumed power in a country that was badly in debt, politically divided, and dependent on the generosity of foreigners. The United States gave Egypt $2.3 billion in aid in 1983.

> *Egypt is now one of the happiest countries in the world. We are not self-supporting. We are still suffering from certain difficulties, from lack of services and in other ways. But because we struggle against the difficulties we are happy. The more you struggle to succeed, the more you take out of life.*
> —ANWAR SADAT
> speaking in 1981

It cannot be denied that Sadat brought about great changes in Egypt and the Middle East, and that he did so very much in the style of modern politics, using the skills of showmanship and publicity. He had worked successfully with the power of images his entire life, using them to rise from a peasant background to a role of world leader and statesman. The fact that he was also seen by some as a traitor does not lessen his stature. He was simply a politician trying hard to deal with the complex problems of the modern world.

One of his last major publicity stunts was a proposal to symbolize the nature of the peace he hoped to achieve for the Middle East. He suggested the construction of a religious complex at the foot of Mount Sinai, containing a mosque, a church, and a synagogue, in the center of which he, Anwar Sadat, peacemaker, would be buried.

Despite Sadat's efforts, the prospects for a lasting peace in the Middle East are still uncertain. The great complex is only a dream, and Anwar Sadat lies buried in a small cemetery outside Cairo.

Ayatollah Ruhollah Khomeini (at left; b. 1900) confers with PLO leader Yassir Arafat (second from left; b. 1929) and Iranian leaders in Tehran. Khomeini's Muslim fundamentalist movement, which overthrew the shah of Iran, has inspired widespread acts of terrorism in the Mideast, including Sadat's assassination.

The funeral procession for Sadat carries his body to the pyramid-shaped Tomb of the Unknown Soldier in suburban Cairo. Combat-ready troops (at lower right) provide tight security for the representatives of 80 countries attending the solemn ceremonies.

Further Reading

Fernandez-Armesto, Felipe. *Sadat and his Statecraft.* London: The Kensal Press, 1982.

Heikal, Mohammed. *Autumn of Fury: The Assassination of Sadat.* New York: Random House, 1983.

Herzog, Chaim. *The Arab-Israeli Wars: War and Peace in the Middle East.* New York: Random House, 1982.

Hurst, David & Irene Beeson. *Sadat.* Winchester, Massachusetts: Faber & Faber, 1982.

Chronology

Dec. 25, 1918	Born Anwar Sadat, in Mit Abul Kom
1936	Enters military academy
1939	Helps found Free Officers Organization
Oct. 1942	Imprisoned by British authorities for participating in abortive attempt by Free Officers to contact commander of Nazi Germany's forces in North Africa
May 15, 1948	Outbreak of first Arab-Israeli War
Jan. 1952	British suppression of Egyptian police garrison at Ismailia triggers rioting throughout the country
July 23, 1952	Sadat announces overthrow of Egyptian monarchy on behalf of Gamal Abdel Nasser and the Free Officers Organization
1956	British, French, and Israeli forces capture Sinai and the Gaza Strip Nasser begins diplomatic offensive to secure Israeli withdrawal
1958	Egypt concludes federation with Syria, thus establishing the United Arab Republic
1960	Federation with Syria discontinued
June 1967	Egypt suffers devastating defeat by Israel in the Six-Day War
1969	Nasser appoints Sadat to the vice-presidency
Sept. 1970	Jordanian expulsion of the Palestine Liberation Organization seriously damages Arab unity Death of Nasser Sadat becomes president of Egypt
1973	Third Arab-Israeli War ends in political and military stalemate
Oct. 1974	Sadat announces *al-Infitah,* a new political and economic initiative designed to attract foreign investment to Egypt
Nov. 1977	Sadat visits Jerusalem for peace talks with Israeli premier Menachem Begin
1978	Sadat and Begin conduct peace negotiations at Camp David, at the invitation of American president James Carter
1979	Peace treaty concluded by Israel and Egypt
Oct. 6, 1981	Anwar Sadat is assassinated by Muslim fundamentalists within the Egyptian armed forces

Index

Patricia Aufderheide is a writer and editor resident in Washington, D.C. She received her Ph.D. in history from the University of Minnesota and has taught the subject both at that university and at the University of Illinois. She is the cultural editor for *In These Times* and has had her work published in such periodicals as *Harper's*, *Newsday*, *The Village Voice*, *American Film*, and *Channels of Communication*.

Arthur M. Schlesinger, jr., taught history at Harvard for many years and is currently Albert Schweitzer Professor of the Humanities at City University of New York. He is the author of numerous highly praised works in American history and has twice been awarded the Pulitzer Prize. He served in the White House as special assistant to presidents Kennedy and Johnson.